OKLAHOMA
ALL-STATE FOOTBALL TEAMS
of the
TWENTIETH CENTURY

Selected by The Oklahoman

Cecil Eugene Reinke

TRAFFORD
PUBLISHING

Order this book online at www.trafford.com
or email orders@trafford.com

Most Trafford titles are also available at major online book retailers.

Printed in the United States of America.

ISBN: 978-1-4669-0776-8 (sc)
ISBN: 978-1-4669-0775-1 (ebk)

Library of Congress Control Number: 2011963400

Trafford rev. 01/26/2012

 www.trafford.com

North America & international
toll-free: 1 888 232 4444 (USA & Canada)
phone: 250 383 6864 ♦ fax: 812 355 4082

 *Dedication*

A friend and classmate, who served forty-one years in the
Armed Forces of the United States of America

SGM William Glen "Bill" Rogers
All-State Guard, *The Daily Oklahoman*, 1951
Clinton High School, Class of 1952

Acknowledgements

Assistance related to this compilation of the All-State teams of the twentieth century, selected by *The Oklahoman,* was provided by the following individuals and high schools: Aaron Alexander, Principal, Heavener; Kathy Atchley, Librarian, Clinton Public Library; Alan Baker, Principal, Cleveland; Brady Barnes, Principal, Hennessey; Bradley R. Bates, Principal, Pryor; Mark Batt, Principal/Athletic Director, Snyder; Jim Beierschmitt, Principal, Enid; Randy Biggs, Principal, Frederick; Ian Brown, Principal, Bristow; Marilyn Buckner, Administrative Assistant to the Principal, Hennessey; Debra Burch, History Teacher, Sperry; George M. Canning, Assistant Principal/Athletic Director, Northwest Classen; Rocky Carter, Athletic Director, El Reno; Lana Park Clark, Class of 1961, Sperry; Cheryl Conditt, Principal, Durant; Danny Crabb, Principal, Sayre; Tom Deighan, Principal, Geary; Cindy Dodds, Principal, Madill; Andrew "Buck" Ewton, Principal, Morris; Beth Edwards, Principal, Chickasha; Doyle Edwards, Principal, Hominy; Randall Esch, Media Specialists, Pawhuska; Kevin Farr, Athletic Historian, Durant; Calypso Gilstrap, Librarian, Norman; Jennifer L. Goldman, Director of Student Services, Oklahoma City Public Schools; Matt Goucher, Principal, El Reno; Steven B. Guy, Sportswriter, *Morris News;* Mark Haught, Principal, Altus; Greg Higgins, Coach, Texhoma; Randy Holley, Superintendent of Public Schools, Shattuck; Jon Holmes, Principal, Tishomingo; Phillip Hoopes, Principal, Garber; Geri Hough, Librarian, Clinton; Boyd Houser, Athletic Director, Tishomingo; Scott Howard, Principal, Northwest Classen; Martha Hudson, Financial Secretary, Chickasha; Jerry Hulme, Principal, Carnegie; Cathy Hunt, Principal, Hobart; Sammy Jackson, Principal, Kingfisher; Michael Jaggars, Superintendent of Public Schools, Wetumka; A. J. Johnson, Chairman, Department of Social Studies, Kingfisher; Chuck Karpe, Principal, Walters; Debra Keil, Principal, Caney Valley; Wayland Kimbie, Principal, Chandler; Kent Lackey, Science Teacher, Henryetta; Kim Lashbrook, Librarian, Bartlesville; Harold LeValley, Principal, Blackwell; Jerri Manning, Principal, Lawton; Pete Maples, Principal, Ryan; Kent Marshall, Principal, Ponca City; Rod Maynard, Principal, Davis; Ladonna Merkel, High School Secretary, Holdenville; Angie

Meservy, Activities Director, Lawton; Scott Morgan, History Teacher, Roff; Lisa Munson, Principal, Miami; Braden Naylor, Principal, Shattuck; Courtney Norton, Librarian, Okmulgee; Ann Palmer, Librarian, Shawnee; James S. Parkhurst, Principal, Alva; Barry Patterson, Athletic Director, Cushing; Rod Pitts, Principal, Pawhuska; Lois Plett, Administrative Secretary, Caney Valley; Matt Posey, Principal, Oilton; Travis Reese, Principal, Mangum; Rick Rogers, Principal, Fairfax; Bobby Rose, Principal, Yale; Kent Roulston, Alumnus, All-State 1979, Wewoka; Mark Shadid, Principal, Weatherford; Bink Stafford, Athletic Director, Madill; Terry Smithey, Registrar, Alva; Dale Spradlin, Principal, Waurika; Gary Stidham, Principal, Konawa; Micheal Thompson, Principal, Deer Creek-Lamont; Kirk Warnick, Principal, Woodward; Marty Webb, Principal, Hollis; Vicki Williams, Family and Consumer Science Teacher, Hominy.

Generous assistance in the compilation of this book was provided by the librarians and the staff of the Al Harris Library, Southwestern Oklahoma State University, Weatherford, where most of the research on this book was accomplished.

Gratitude is extended to *The Oklahoman*, one of the great newspapers of the United States, for making copies of all past published editions available on film to the Oklahoma Historical Society, and to all the colleges and universities of Oklahoma.

Special appreciation is extended to Randy Biggs, Principal, Frederick High School, for providing the photograph of Lewis "Chicken" Pope, All-State Fullback, 1926, that appears on the front cover of this book.

C. E. R.

Explanation By Cecil Eugene Reinke

This is a history book.

The purpose of writing a history book is to see that the past is remembered, remembered correctly, and remembered as fully as the writer can make possible.

The history of Oklahoma high school All-State team selections by *The Daily Oklahoman*, now designated *The Oklahoman*, has evaded many of the most devoted Oklahoma high school football fans and supporters. Ironically, the reason this history is not known by fans and supporters is that, apparently, it is not known by *The Oklahoman*.

Concurrent with announcement of *The Daily Oklahoman* All-State team of 1937, the newspaper published a list of earlier selections, starting with the team of 1925, under the caption "All-State Grid Players Since the 1925 Campaign." The published list recorded the names of first team choices only, ignorant of or indifferent to the fact that the newspaper had selected a first, second, third, and fourth team in 1925; a first and a second team in 1926; and first, second and third teams in 1927, 1928, 1929, 1930, 1931, 1932, 1933, 1934, 1935, 1936, and 1937. Why the writer of this article went back only to the year 1925 one can only speculate. Possibly, the reporter thought that the selection of All-State high school teams by the Daily Oklahoman started in 1925, or, possibly, he thought selections of years earlier than 1925 would be of no interest to readers.

In an article accompanying announcement of the 1945 All-State team, under the heading "44 Schools on '45 All-State," a Daily Oklahoman correspondent wrote, "Here is a tonic-and-bitters for despondent college football coaches, a remedy guaranteed to cure the most severe case of gridiron ennui – The Daily Oklahoman's twenty-first annual All-State high school football team, cream of the 1945 prep school pigskin parade and bigger and faster than ever – 44 players from as many schools in all sections of the state."

The newspaper that announced the 1945 All-State team included a list of former Daily Oklahoman All-State teams, starting with the year 1925. In recording the teams of 1925 through 1937, the newspaper counted on each team only eleven men, incorrectly believing that in each of those years only one eleven-man team had been named. For years 1938 through 1944, the listing correctly reported that in each of these years the newspaper selected forty-four players on an equal basis, without assignments to first, second, third, and fourth teams. The newspaper explicitly confirmed lack of knowledge relating to when selections began, and numbers of players named on the All-State teams selected prior to 1938: "Here is the Star-Spangled review of All-Staters of the past. Starting in 1925, only 11 men were selected, but since 1937, 44 players have been named in North-South squads for Oklahoma's all-star game in Oklahoma City."

Obviously, the sportswriter believed that the selection of high school All-State teams by the Daily Oklahoman began in 1925. In fact, selections began with the team of 1913. Equally apparent is that the sportswriter believed the teams of 1925 through 1937 each consisted of only eleven players. Actually, the All-State squad of 1925 consisted of forty-four players, assigned to first, second, third, and fourth teams. The All-State squad of 1926 included twenty-two players, a first and a second team. The All-State selections of years 1927 through 1937 each consisted of thirty-three players, assigned to three teams.

These errors are repeated periodically concurrent with All-State announcements.

The practice of selecting Oklahoma high school All-State football teams was started by *The Daily Oklahoman*, published in Oklahoma City, in year 1913. That year, the newspaper published the first to be named All-State team, designated the "OKLAHOMA ALL-STAR HIGH SCHOOL ELEVEN," chosen by newspaper sportswriters. T*he Daily Oklahoman*, later designated *The Oklahoman*, selected a high school All-State team every remaining year of the twentieth century, and beyond.

Regrettably, from a research point of view, between 1913, the first year an All-State team was selected, and 1937, players selected were identified by last names, surnames, only. This was presumably adequate identification at the times, with smaller schools and a lower state population, but is inadequate for historical identifications.

I wrote to almost all of the Oklahoma high schools involved, asking their help in ascertaining the first names of players identified by surnames only, and received generous responses. All first names that have become known are herein added.

One of the high school principals I wrote called me to inquire why someone living in Oregon would be writing a book about Oklahoma high school football. I explained that while my home is in Portland, Oregon, my hometown is Clinton,

Oklahoma, and that I had played three years of high school football. "So, you were a Red Tornado," he exclaimed. I was pleased that he knew the name of my hometown team. Then he asked, "What year were you an All-Stater?" I quickly corrected this assumption; "I wasn't an All-Stater. I wasn't even close to being an All-Stater." I emphasized that I was not writing a book about me, that this was not a book of self-aggrandizement. I explained that while I played three years of high school football, even saying that I "played" is somewhat of a stretch. In my three years, I was never a member of what we then referred to as the "first team." I was always a substitute, awarded a school letter only as a senior. But I did practice with and from "the best seat in the house" I watched the talented play of four Daily Oklahoman all-state selections – Guard Raymond Jantz and Halfback Duane Reed in 1949, End Bob LaRue in 1950, and Guard Bill Rogers in 1951.

One intent of this book is to provide for Oklahoma high school football fans, including former players, those named to All-State teams and those not, opportunity for moments of reminiscence. Perhaps some gentleman now in his eighties will look and proclaim, "Hey, I played against that guy, and he was an all-stater." Perhaps some young woman now attending high school will read the names and say, "I've always heard that my grandfather was an all-state tackle in high school; now I know it's true." Hopefully, there will be some son of a one of the men selected in 1942 delighted with confirmation that his father was on the same All-State team as Bob Fenimore.

Another intent is to encourage readers to wonder, as I do, how those men selected on All-State teams fared in life after high school football. A troublesome question in my mind: *The Daily Oklahoman* All-State team of 1941 was announced on Sunday, December 7, Pearl Harbor day. Doubtless, most of those young men, if not all, served in our Armed Forces during World War II. How many of them came home to Oklahoma?

Those who went on to gain fame as college players, or achieve stardom in professional football, many know about. Many, avid fans can name them, became All-Americans. Three twentieth century selections – Billy Vessels, Cleveland, 1948; Steve Owens, Miami, 1965; and Jason White, Tuttle, 1997 and 1998 – won the Heisman.

Darrell Royal, Hollis, 1942; and Mike Gundy, Midwest City, 1985, gained recognition and the respect of football fans everywhere as college football coaches.

J. C. Watts, Eufaula, 1975, became a respected Congressman.

Bennie L. Davis, McAlester, 1945, rose to become a four-star General, and the Commander in Chief of the United States Air Force Strategic Air Command.

Equally to be respected, if not more so, are those who served their nation, state, and communities without widespread recognition. I think of Brad Bates, Pryor, 1974, who after college returned to his home town where for twenty-two years he taught Industrial/Technology Education at Pryor Junior High School, coaching football for seventeen of those years. He served five years the Assistant Principal of Pryor High School. Now he is the Principal of Pryor High School. Likewise, I think of Bill Beierschmitt, Alva, 1962, the Provost and Chief Operating Officer of the Bartlesville campus of Rogers State University, who earlier in his thirty-plus years career served as a teacher, a Middle School Principal, a Mid-High School Principal, a High School Principal, and the Superintendent of Schools, in the Bartlesville public school system. These men, and numerous other All-State high school football players, are to be lauded for careers dedicated to the education of the young men and women of Oklahoma.

No criticism of any sportswriter for not knowing when the Daily Oklahoman first started selecting high school All-State football teams, or for not knowing the number of players selected on All-State teams prior to 1938, is intended. The job of a newspaper sportswriter is to report what happens in sports, and this the sportswriters for *The Daily Oklahoman*, now designated *The Oklahoman*, have done and continue to do, accurately and interestingly. What is intended is recognition that it was *The Daily Oklahoman* that began the practice of naming high school All-State football teams in Oklahoma.

What the compiler of this book wants to see, in the year 2012, is a sports headline that reads something like: "This is it! The 100th Oklahoman All-State Team."

OKLAHOMA

OKLAHOMA

TWENTIETH CENTURY HIGH SCHOOL
ALL–STATE FOOTBALL TEAMS

Selected by *The Oklahoman*

OKLAHOMA ALL-STATE FOOTBALL TEAM: 1913

Name	School	Position
Thomas O. Mitcher	Oklahoma City	Left End
Paul McFerron	Norman	Left Tackle
Charles Higgins	Shawnee	Left Guard
P. Austin Wallace	Oklahoma City	Center
Creamer	Tulsa	Right Guard
Claude M. Tyler	Oklahoma City	Right Tackle
Dawson	Tulsa	Right End
John Young	Tulsa	Quarterback
Charles Swatek	Oklahoma City	Left Halfback
Edward Capshaw	Norman	Right Halfback
John Baumgarner	Norman	Fullback

OKLAHOMA ALL-STATE FOOTBALL TEAM: 1914

FIRST TEAM

Name	School	Position
George Abbott	Norman	Left End
Bernard	Cherokee	Left Tackle
Richard Barker	Oklahoma City	Left Guard
Dall	Cherokee	Center
Claude McGlothin	Shawnee	Right Guard
Claude M. Tyler	Oklahoma City	Right Tackle
DeLos Detar	Oklahoma City	Right End
Edward Karbusicky	Oklahoma City	Quarterback
Wayne McCorkle	Oklahoma City	Left Halfback
King Faucett	Shawnee	Right Halfback
James Johnson	Norman	Fullback

SECOND TEAM

Name	School	Position
Percy Porter	Enid	Left End
Charles Higgins	Shawnee	Left Tackle
Dodson	Oklahoma City	Left Guard
Leigh A. Wallace	Oklahoma City	Center
McBeth	Oklahoma City	Right Guard
Harry Bass	Enid	Right Tackle
Wallace Abbott	Norman	Right End
Degraffenreid	Muskogee	Quarterback
Gus Hamilton	Chickasha	Left Halfback
Warren Meeks	Shawnee	Right Halfback
Carr	Oklahoma City	Fullback

OKLAHOMA ALL-STATE FOOTBALL TEAM: 1915

FIRST TEAM

Name	School	Position
Millspaugh	Cherokee	Left End
Chester Capshaw	Norman	Left Tackle
Young	Tulsa	Left Guard
Leigh A. Wallace	Oklahoma City	Center
John Hirt	Pawhuska	Right Guard
DeLos Detar	Oklahoma City	Right Tackle
Erwn Poole	Chickasha	Right End
Thomas O. Mitcher	Oklahoma City	Quarterback
Wallace Abbott	Norman	Left Halfback
Edward Karbusicky	Oklahoma City	Right Halfback
"Skinny" Davis	Norman	Fullback

SECOND TEAM

Name	School	Position
Charles Parsons	Oklahoma City	Left End
Hale	Cherokee	Left Tackle
Miller	Cherokee	Left Guard
Dall	Cherokee	Center
Wales	Norman	Right Guard
King Faucett	Shawnee	Right Tackle
Thurman Meek	Shawnee	Right End
William Wicker	Enid	Quarterback
Coldiron	Cherokee	Left Halfback
John Comstock	Pawhuska	Right Halfback
Hafer	Cherokee	Fullback

OKLAHOMA ALL-STATE FOOTBALL TEAM: 1916

FIRST TEAM

Name	School	Position
Snake Arbuckle	Madill	End
Rudy Comstock	Pawhuska	Tackle
Pliny Newbern	Oklahoma City	Guard
Clark	Tecumseh	Center
Foster	Norman	Guard
Walls	Norman	Tackle
Clyde Leforce	Blackwell	End
Kiefer	Tulsa	Quarterback
Wallace Abbott	Norman	Halfback
John Comstock	Pawhuska	Halfback
Everett Hafer	Blackwell	Fullback

SECOND TEAM

Name	School	Position
Skaggs	Norman	End
Grey	Norman	Tackle
William Marion	Pawhuska	Guard
Ernest M. Harkins	Oklahoma City	Center
Chauncey Goetting	Chickasha	Guard
Young	Tulsa	Tackle
G. Myron Tyler	Oklahoma City	End
Russell D. Hardy	Oklahoma City	Quarterback
Houston Hill	Chickasha	Halfback
Meeks	Shawnee	Halfback
Harold Burt	Pawhuska	Fullback

OKLAHOMA ALL-STATE FOOTBALL TEAM: 1917

FIRST TEAM

Name	School	Wt.	Position
Shorty Marsh	Madill	150	Left End
Norris	Cherokee	170	Left Tackle
Joe Milam	Cherokee	167	Left Guard
Dow Hamm	Muskogee	178	Center
Elmer Wails	Norman	160	Right Guard
W. Williams	Marshall	171	Right Tackle
G. Myron Tyler	Oklahoma City	154	Right End
Russell D. Hardy	Oklahoma City	128	Quarterback
W. Wilson	Marshall	150	Left Halfback
White	Oklahoma City	170	Right Halfback
Robert Winkler	Bartlesville	155	Fullback

SECOND TEAM

Name	School	Position
Roy J. Garner	Oklahoma City	Left End
George A. Cole	Oklahoma City	Left Tackle
Robert Howard	Norman	Left Guard
Charley Dunlap	Ponca City	Center
Burris	Mountain View	Right Guard
Frank Proctor	Bartlesville	Right Tackle
Roy Gray	Bartlesville	Right End
Walter Dowler	Bartlesville	Quarterback
Brandt	Cherokee	Left Halfback
Hopping	Tulsa	Right Halfback
Roy "Mike" Swatek	Oklahoma City	Fullback

THIRD TEAM

Name	School	Position
Lotton	Cherokee	Left End
Harkleroad	Ponca City	Left Tackle
William McKenzie	Madill	Left Guard
Neil Dixon	Bartlesville	Center
Morgan	Enid	Right Guard
Dickinson	Tulsa	Right Tackle
Fibus	Shawnee	Right End
Meeks	Shawnee	Quarterback
Herschel A. Graham	Oklahoma City	Left Halfback
Houston Hill	Chickasha	Right Halfback
Slaight	Muskogee	Fullback

OKLAHOMA ALL-STATE FOOTBALL TEAM: 1918

Name	School	Position
M. Eugene Meister	Oklahoma City	Left End
Gassoway	Stillwater	Left Tackle
Hoffman	Shawnee	Left Guard
Howard Richards	Enid	Center
Lee Jackson	Shawnee	Right Guard
Robert Howard	Norman	Right Tackle
Tom Taylor	Norman	Right End
Barry "Poke" Harsh	Ponca City	Quarterback
Roy J. Garner	Oklahoma City	Left Halfback
Carl E. Schlabach	Oklahoma City	Right Halfback
Earl W. Hendricks	Oklahoma City	Fullback

OKLAHOMA ALL-STATE FOOTBALL TEAM: 1919

FIRST TEAM

Name	School	Position
Weeks	Cherokee	Left End
Homer Maudlin	Fairfax	Left Tackle
J. Rowan Talliaferro	Oklahoma City	Left Guard
Bentley Sears	Bristow	Center
Lee Jackson	Shawnee	Right Guard
Clifford Bowles	Norman	Right Tackle
M. Eugene Meister	Oklahoma City	Right End
Hendrix	Tulsa	Quarterback
Orr	Ada	Left Halfback
Miller	Muskogee	Right Halfback
Earl W. Hendricks	Oklahoma City	Fullback

SECOND TEAM

Name	School	Position
Ray Windham	El Reno	Left End
Tracy A. Robertson	Oklahoma City	Left Tackle
Forrest Robinson	Okmulgee	Left Guard
Sherer	Cherokee	Center
Abe Voth	Enid	Right Guard
Clark Trent	Okmulgee	Right Tackle
Tom Taylor	Norman	Right End
Emmett Foley	Fairfax	Quarterback
Schlabach	Oklahoma City	Left Halfback
Mason	Guthrie	Right Halfback
Clyde "Shang" Herndon	Lawton	Fullback

THIRD TEAM

Name	School	Position
Wittenberg	Stillwater	Left End
Justin Gevers	Lawton	Left Tackle
Jernigan	Blackwell	Left Guard
Smith	Carnegie	Center
White	Muskogee	Right Guard
Stanley Driskill	Chickasha	Right Tackle
Oliver	Ada	Right End
Earl Jones	Blackwell	Quarterback
George Washington	Roff	Left Halfback
Barton	Muskogee	Right Halfback
Hasbrook	Enid	Fullback

OKLAHOMA ALL-STATE FOOTBALL TEAM: 1920

FIRST TEAM

Name	School	Position
Swanson	Muskogee	End
Weeks	Cherokee	End
Montgomery	Muskogee	Tackle
Bascum Pippin	Lawton	Tackle
Forrest Robinson	Okmulgee	Guard
Ted Schlotterbeck	Chickasha	Guard
Clifford Gigoux	Lawton	Center
Morris	Sapulpa	Quarterback
Hughes	Tulsa	Halfback
Carl E. Schlabach	Oklahoma City	Halfback
Penny	Muskogee	Fullback

SECOND TEAM

Name	School	Position
Locke	Norman	End
Clarence Rader	Lamont	End
Lee Jackson	Shawnee	Tackle
Henderson	Cherokee	Tackle
Dowis Dyer	Blackwell	Guard
Herschel Crow	Altus	Guard
White	Muskogee	Center
Box	Notowa	Quarterback
Carl Hanks	Lawton	Halfback
William Fly	Fairfax	Halfback
Diamond Roach	Chickasha	Fullback

OKLAHOMA ALL-STATE FOOTBALL TEAM: 1921

FIRST TEAM	POSITION	SECOND TEAM
Floyd H. McBride, Oklahoma City	End	Rader, Lamont
Josie Hickman, Altus	End	King, Pauls Valley
Jones, Sapulpa	Tackle	Boop, Nowata
Gross, Guthrie	Tackle	Joe Nash, Fairfax
Johnson, Pond Creek	Guard	L. Caywood, Sapulpa
Parrish, Nowata	Guard	Quilter, Tulsa
Davidson, Ardmore	Center	Clifford Gigoux, Lawton
Thomas, Sapulpa	Quarter	Slough, Ardmore
Morris, Sapulpa	Halfback	Sullivan, Ardmore
Dale Arbuckle, Enid	Halfback	Bernard A. Hunter, Oklahoma City
Sheehan, Tulsa	Fullback	Pete Kimberlin, Altus

THIRD TEAM	POSITION	FOURTH TEAM
Burdick, Goltry	End	Dyer, Sapulpa
Billy Campbell, Shawnee	End	Frank Crider, Durant
McCrady, Sapulpa	Tackle	John Everett, Enid
Charles Comstock, Pawhuska	Tackle	Loren "Snooks" Martin, Norman
Potter, Marshall	Guard	William R. Wolfe, Oklahoma City
Hugh Hanshaw, Clinton	Guard	Clyde Fleming, Norman
Robert Mastin, Wetumka	Center	Roy Davis, Kingfisher
Ticer, Carnegie	Quarter	Gaskill, Perry
George Beaulieu, Pawhuska	Halfback	Hutson, El Reno
Roy Miller, Hobart	Halfback	Dave "Buck" Meeks, Shawnee
Bean, Nowata	Fullback	McAlister, Sapulpa

OKLAHOMA ALL-STATE FOOTBALL TEAM: 1922

FIRST TEAM

Name	School	Position
Harry Braden	Blackwell	End
Brown	Ardmore	End
McCrady	Sapulpa	Tackle
Harold Weissinger	Enid	Tackle
Gross	Guthrie	Guard
John Okley Maberry	Sayre	Guard
Charles W. Hughes	Oklahoma City	Center
Ledford	Tulsa	Quarterback
Lynwood "Bus" Haskins	Enid	Halfback
Robert "Bob" Lee	Ramona	Halfback
Diamond Roach	Chickasha	Fullback

SECOND TEAM

Name	School	Position
Ikie Peace	Altus	End
Jennings	Muskogee	End
Charles Comstock	Pawhuska	Tackle
Jones	Sapulpa	Tackle
Mike Brewer	Bristow	Guard
Owen Nott	Oklahoma City	Guard
Hardie	Tulsa	Center
Marshal Covin	Clinton	Quarterback
Potts	Ada	Halfback
Willingham	Ardmore	Halfback
Pipkins	Eufaula	Fullback

OKLAHOMA ALL-STATE FOOTBALL TEAM: 1923

FIRST TEAM	POSITION	SECOND TEAM
Frank Crider, Durant	End	Markowitz, Tulsa
Brown, Ardmore	End	Hamilton, Ardmore
Moore, Tulsa	Tackle	Walter Cramer, Blackwell
Bollard Williamson, Clinton	Tackle	White, Nowata
Roy Poteet, Guthrie	Guard	Ross Anderson, Pryor
Dale Roush, Blackwell	Guard	Zeman, Redford
Otto Simma, Cushing	Center	Smith, Sapulpa
Lynwood "Bus" Haskins, Enid	Quarter	Bennett Storey, Durant
Dwight Funk, Oklahoma City	Halfback	Bullet, Dewey
Leon "Jelly" Vinson, Shawnee	Halfback	Tyler McDonald, El Reno
Lester Caywood, Sapulpa	Fullback	Pipkins, Eufauia

THIRD TEAM	POSITON	FOURTH TEAM
Joseph LeCrone, Bristow	End	John Myers, Blackwell
Wood, Perry	End	Lee McMahan, Fairfax
George "Al" Keller, Woodward	Tackle	McCombs, Eufaula
George W. Brunner, Oklahoma City	Tackle	Johnson, Pond Creek
Owen, McAlister	Guard	George Webber, Henryetta
Drain, Tulsa	Guard	Kenneth Cramer, Blackwell
Bill Hale, Altus	Center	Kelley, Tulsa
Grimes, Tulsa	Quarter	Wender, Weatherford
Selby, Tulsa	Halfback	Austin Bond, Chickasha
Hurt, Eufaula	Halfback	Crater, Muskogee
Chet "Pood" McClain, Alva	Fullback	Kent, Perry

OKLAHOMA ALL-STATE FOOTBALL TEAM: 1924

FIRST TEAM

Name	School	Position
Edward Aughtry	Oklahoma City	End
Clarence Frost	Norman	End
Roy Poteet	Guthrie	Tackle
Harvey Sark	Bartlesville	Tackle
Dale Roush	Blackwell	Guard
Edgar "Bally" Madison	Sayre	Guard
Shiflett	Wewoka	Center
Ingraham	Tulsa	Quarterback
Joe Fuquay	Stigler	Halfback
Secrest	McAlister	Halfback
Ward	Muskogee	Fullback

SECOND TEAM

John Brooks	Tulsa	End
Emmet McLean	Enid	End
Louis Bernier	Norman	Tackle
Hugh Cunningham	Oklahoma City	Tackle
Bill Drain	Tulsa	Guard
Okla Paden	Geary	Guard
Crowder	Carnegie	Center
Lewis Miller	Blackwell	Quarterback
Sheldon Blackman	Claremore	Halfback
Thomas	Drumright	Halfback
Otis Flint	Kingfisher	Fullback

THIRD TEAM

Steve Redfern	Ponca City	End
Jack Carmen	Bristow	End
Charles Johnson	Pond Creek	Tackle
McDaniel	Stigler	Tackle
Ralph Wolfe	Oklahoma City	Guard
Denver Watts	Morris	Guard
R. Fails	Cherokee	Center
Eaglechief	Pawnee	Quarterback
Denny McAnerny	Sayre	Halfback
Tipton	Wilson	Halfback
Eubanks	Fairview	Fullback

ALL–OKLAHOMA HIGH SCHOOL TEAMS: 1925

FIRST TEAM	POSITION	SECOND TEAM
Jack Carmen, Bristow	End	McCrosky, Oklahoma City
Laurence Krueger, Henryetta	End	Johnson, Yukon
Harvey Sark, Bartlesville	Tackle	Cawood, Nash
Kenneth Cramer, Blackwell	Tackle	Walter Grapes, Ponca City
McCord, Wilson	Guard	Dunlap, McAlester
Ralph Cochran, Kingfisher	Guard	Dale Hamilton, Bristow
Kelly, Tulsa	Center	Adams, Weatherford
Harold L. Pickens, Oklahoma City	Quarterback	Charles Stogner, Norman
Guy Warren, Norman	Halfback	Ward Lynn, Fairfax
Hinson, Muskogee	Halfback	Foley, Eufaula
O'Leary, McAlester	Fullback	Harry Smith, Bartlesville

THIRD TEAM	POSITION	FOURTH TEAM
Pate, OC Classen	End	Harry Sinderson, Enid
Tarver, McAlester	End	H. Eubanks, Fairview
Clarence Royce, El Reno	Tackle	Frank Yires, Notowa
Roy "Slim" Burnett, Ryan	Tackle	Rodman, Sapulpa
Clyde Kirk, Norman	Guard	Glen Bailey, Chickasha
Lyle Brandt, Shawnee	Guard	Barnes, Muskogee
White, Muskogee	Center	Smith, Supulpa
Wilson, Cherokee	Quarterback	Moore "Bodie" Williams, Cleveland
Wallace Caywood, Bristow	Halfback	Al Fields, Morris
Earl Flint, Kingfisher	Halfback	McGee, Cherokee
Sheldon Blackman, Claremore	Fullback	Frost, Norman

OKLAHOMA ALL-STATE FOOTBALL TEAM: 1926

FIRST TEAM

Name	School	Position
Bruce Jones	Bartlesville	End
Jack Runsom	Eufaula	End
Frank Yiram	Nowata	Tackle
Doyle Tolleson	Norman	Tackle
Lawrence Hildenbrand	Ponca City	Guard
John Newell	Yale	Guard
Lloyd Roberts	Stigler	Center
Jay Thomas	Chickasha	Quarterback
Bill Robb	Oklahoma City	Halfback
Earl Flint	Kingfisher	Halfback
John Daugherty	Purcell	Fullback

SECOND TEAM

Jake Knight	McAlester	End
Doug Elam	OC Capital Hill	End
Stone	Tecumseh	Tackle
Howard Lamb	Henryetta	Tackle
Jack Blanton	Norman	Guard
Fred Miles	Pawhuska	Guard
Stenbee	Oklahoma City	Center
Ted Hand	OC Classen	Quarterback
Highfill	Cherokee	Halfback
Fred Smith	Blackwell	Halfback
Lewis "Chicken" Pope	Frederick	Fullback

OKLAHOMA ALL-STATE FOOTBALL TEAM: 1927

FIRST TEAM

Name	School	Position
David "Steve" Stevens	Okmulgee	End
Leo Howard	Tulsa	End
Ray Hillis	Lawton	Tackle
Howard Lamb	Henryetta	Tackle
John Newell	Yale	Guard
William S. "Bill" Oates	Oklahoma City	Guard
Dale Hamilton	Bristow	Center
Reginald Walker	Blackwell	Quarterback
Tony Kirkegard	Yukon	Halfback
Jay Thomas	Chickasha	Halfback
Pete Nance	Hollis	Fullback

SECOND TEAM

Bob Carter	Blackwell	End
Yates	Haskell	End
Frank Pearce	Nowata	Tackle
Baker	Picher	Tackle
Bishop	Muskogee	Guard
Wesley Wilson	Enid	Guard
James Hort	Perkins	Center
R. Anderson	Ardmore	Quarterback
Harry Stone	Jet	Halfback
Deberry	Wilson	Halfback
John C. Soergel	Oklahoma City	Fullback

THIRD TEAM

Lofton Reynolds	Altus	End
Piper	Pawnee	End
Maloney	Guthrie	Tackle
Huhn	Blackwell	Tackle
Jo Jo Anderson	Ardmore	Guard
Douglas Wright	Lawton	Guard
Gilbrenth	Grandfield	Center
Thompson	Wetumka	Quarterback
Perrin	Covington	Halfback
Pilkington	Collinsville	Halfback
Denver Harrelson	Blackwell	Fullback

OKLAHOMA ALL-STATE FOOTBALL TEAM: 1928

FIRST TEAM

Name	School	Position
Fred Cherry	Okmulgee	End
Lloyd Yates	Haskell	End
Joe Wright	Duncan	Tackle
Bill Baker	Picher	Tackle
George Hoffman	Okmulgee	Guard
Vernie Volger	Yale	Guard
Phil Young	Norman	Center
Sidney "Blondy" Clark	Shawnee	Quarterback
John C. Soergel	OC Central	Halfback
Harry Stone	Jet	Halfback
Ormand "Dilly" Beach	Pawhuska	Fullback

SECOND TEAM

Nall	Jet	End
Ben Frans	Clinton	End
Maloney	Guthrie	Tackle
Roye	Stigler	Tackle
Smith	Claremore	Guard
Wilson	OC Central	Guard
Sherwood	Rush Springs	Center
Weaver	Muskogee	Quarterback
Barham	Dundee	Halfback
Hildinger	Nash	Halfback
Julian Bowden	Wetumka	Fullback

THIRD TEAM

Keller	OC Capitol Hill	End
Armitage	Carnegie	End
Frank McGuire	Bartlesville	Tackle
Criswell	Purcell	Tackle
Ellis Bashara	Norman	Guard
Cherry	Anadarko	Guard
Burchfiel	Nash	Center
Monenger	Yukon	Quarterback
Doyle Lawson	Idabel	Halfback
Robertson	Seminole	Halfback
Maloney	OC Classen	Fullback

OKLAHOMA ALL-STATE FOOTBALL TEAM: 1929

FIRST TEAM

Name	School	Pos.	Ht.	Wt.	Age	Class
Goetting	Wewoka	E	6-4	185	17	Senior
Paul Early	Ponca City	E	5-11	160	18	Senior
George B. Wheeler	Davis	T	6-2	196	18	Senior
Harley Kersey	Okmulgee	T	5-11	185	18	Senior
Henry Haag	Norman	G	6-0	185	19	Senior
Douglas Wright	Lawton	G	5-9	170	19	Senior
Wendell "Lefty" List	Bristow	C	5-11	180	17	Senior
Roy "Skeet" Berry	Shawnee	QB	5-10	156	17	Senior
Pete Maloney	OC Classen	HB	6-0	168	19	Senior
Jeff King	Wagoner	HB	5-10	195	20	Senior
Holt	Guthrie	FB	6-1	175	20	Senior

SECOND TEAM

Name	School	Position
Eugene Tims	Bartlesville	End
Claude Richardson	Fairfax	End
Kenneth Oringderff	Enid	Tackle
Ed Skelton	Shawnee	Tackle
Ellis Bashara	Norman	Guard
Leonald Noel	Blackwell	Guard
Kuhn	Carnegie	Center
Marshall	Weatherford	Quarterback
Everett Starnes	Guthrie	Halfback
Cash Gentry	Lawton	Halfback
Cal Clemens	OC Central	Fullback

THIRD TEAM

Barton	OC Capitol Hill	End
Ralph Anderson	Okmulgee	End
Paul Gardner	El Reno	Tackle
Lyle Nunn	Hobart	Tackle
T. Ray Phillips	OC Classen	Guard
O. C. Lassiter	Shawnee	Guard
Ralph Hickman	OC Central	Center
Robertson	Seminole	Quarterback
Herchel Martin	Ponca City	Halfback
Leonard "PeeWee" McFee	Hominy	Halfback
J. G. Kitchen	Okmulgee	Fullback

OKLAHOMA ALL-STATE FOOTBALL TEAM: 1930

FIRST TEAM

Name	School	Pos.	Ht.	Wt.	Age	Class
Allen Holt	Purcell	E	6-1	178	18	Senior
Eugene Tims	Bartlesville	E	6-2	182	18	Senior
Charles Jones	Muskogee	T	5-11	178	20	Senior
Ed Skelton	Shawnee	T	6-1	190	18	Junior
Rudolph Prochaska	Medford	G	5-9	176	20	Senior
T. Ray Phillips	OC Classen	G	5-10	162	19	Senior
Bud Wilkes	Ardmore	C	6-4	210	19	Senior
Omar Browning	Enid	QB	5-10	147	18	Senior
Ernest Bullette	Dewar	HB	6-0	160	18	Junior
Cecil Byrns	Frederick	HB	5-9	190	20	Senior
Leonard McFee	Pawhuska	FB	6-0	175	18	Senior

SECOND TEAM

Name	School	Position
Jess Ferrell	Lawton	End
Horton	Hugo	End
J. W. "Red" Stacy	Altus	Tackle
Gardner	OC Classen	Tackle
John Coody	Tulsa	Guard
Lewis Horany	Cushing	Guard
Duane Lance	Ponca City	Center
Robertson	Seminole	Quarterback
Everett McElreach	Muskogee	Halfback
Frank Whaley	Shawnee	Halfback
Manuels	Pond Creek	Fullback

THIRD TEAM

Rudy Cotton	Mangum	End
Pope	Frederick	End
Harley Kersey	Okmulgee	Tackle
Edwin Porter	El Reno	Tackle
Robert Kee	Hennessey	Guard
Martin	Marlow	Guard
Cecil McDaniels	Lawton	Center
Craig	Pauls Valley	Quarterback
Roy Lee Dawson	Chandler	Halfback
Kester Trent	Heavener	Halfback
Flow	Chickasha	Fullback

OKLAHOMA ALL-STATE FOOTBALL TEAM: 1931

FIRST TEAM

Name	School	Pos.	Ht.	Wt.	Age	Class
Jess Ferrell	Lawton	E	5-11	170	18	Senior
Sanford Newsom	Yukon	E	5-10	150	17	Junior
Bob Reynolds	Okmulgee	T	6-4	210	17	Senior
Ed Skelton	Shawnee	T	6-1	190	20	Senior
Ernest "Bud" Kee	Hennessey	G	6-0	190	18	Senior
Fred DeMier	Miami	G	5-10	190	18	Senior
Orville Tuttle	Bartlesville	C	5-11	175	18	Senior
Karey Fuqua	Lawton	QB	5-10	162	18	Senior
Jack Fleming	OC Classen	HB	5-9	165	18	Senior
Webber Merrell	Guthrie	HB	5-11	160	18	Senior
Jack Harris	Antlers	FB	6-1	180	17	Senior

SECOND TEAM

Name	School	Position
Edwards	Broken Bow	End
Cox	Muskogee	End
Lester "Red" Chapman	Hollis	Tackle
Bill Breeden	OC Central	Tackle
Platt	Wagoner	Guard
Casey	OC Classen	Guard
Coates	Duncan	Center
Weber	Newkirk	Quarterback
Nim Newberry	Lawton	Halfback
Frank Whaley	Shawnee	Halfback
Jack Sweet	OC Classen	Fullback

THIRD TEAM

Name	School	Position
Harold Burress	Blackwell	End
Barney Hale	Texhoma	End
Mike Montgomery	Lawton	Tackle
Clair Gregg	Garber	Tackle
Lewis Horany	Cushing	Guard
Briggs	Cleveland	Guard
James Schneider	Pawhuska	Center
Bloomfield	Tulsa	Quarterback
Young	Picher	Halfback
Gordon "Cake" Gore	Clinton	Halfback
Poynor	Weleetka	Fullback

OKLAHOMA ALL–STATE FOOTBALL TEAM: 1932

FIRST TEAM

Name	School	Pos.	WT.	Ht.	Age	Class
Harry Allen	Tulsa Central	E	187	6-2	19	Senior
Raymond Martin	Broken Bow	E	190	6-3	19	Senior
Lester Chapman	Hollis	T	185	6-2	18	Senior
Herbert Ferrell	OC Capitol Hill	T	178	6-1	19	Senior
Aubrey Anthony	Shawnee	G	175	5-10	19	Senior
Lester Graham	Hominy	G	190	5-11	18	Senior
Mickey Parks	Shawnee	C	210	5-11	17	Senior
Lloyd Jones	Muskogee	QB	165	5-8	17	Junior
Clarence Phillips	Bristow	HB	175	6-1	18	Senior
Jimmie Cain	Holdenville	HB	183	5-10	20	Senior
Frank Henderson	McAlester	FB	167	5-10	19	Junior

SECOND TEAM

Player	School	Position
Newsom	Yukon	End
Joe Osborne	Miami	End
Connie Ahrens	OC Classen	Tackle
Roy Gilliam	Chandler	Tackle
George Anderson	Clinton	Guard
Chesbro	Haskins	Guard
Conkright	Tulsa	Center
Walcott	OC Capitol Hill	Quarterback
Merrell	Guthrie	Halfback
Jack Choate	Hennessey	Halfback
Orville Mathews	Chickasha	Fullback

THIRD TEAM

Cutchall	OC Classen	End
Asbury	McAlester	End
Joe Lemonds	Durant	Tackle
Lowell S. Montgomery	Walters	Tackle
Anderson	Sulphur	Guard
Mark Hodgson	Ponca City	Guard
E. O. Billingslea	Frederick	Center
Baer	Shawnee	Quarterback
Page	Jet	Halfback
Nix	Purcell	Halfback
West	Dundee	Fullback

OKLAHOMA ALL-STATE FOOTBALL TEAM: 1933

FIRST TEAM

Name	School	Pos.	Wt.	Ht.	Age	Class
Leo Goodrum	Duncan	E	155	5-11	19	Senior
Zack Smith	Frederick	E	170	6-1	18	Senior
Lynn Marsh	Durant	T	195	6-2	19	Senior
John Schellestede	Blackwell	T	220	6-4	20	Senior
Lester Graham	Hominy	G	190	5-11	19	Senior
Harold Griffith	Hugo	G	158	5-10	17	Senior
Bruce Long	OC Capitol Hill	C	175	5-11	17	Senior
Lloyd Jones	Muskogee	QB	170	5-8	18	Senior
Orville Mathews	Chickasha	HB	155	5-11	18	Senior
Raphael Boudreau	Purcell	HB	168	5-10	19	Senior
Crusty Barton	OC Capitol Hill	FB	155	5-11	19	Senior

SECOND TEAM

Name	School	Position
Virgil Salmon	Henryetta	End
Ray Webba	OC Central	End
Wyrick	OC Capitol Hill	Tackle
J. L. Jones	Muskogee	Tackle
Beaver	OC Capitol Hill	Guard
Ed Thompson	Shawnee	Guard
Billie Bennett	Snyder	Center
Barr	Shawnee	Quarterback
Fred Sims	OC Classen	Halfback
Crowder	Cherokee	Halfback
Roach	Waurika	Fullback

THIRD TEAM

Ed Cheek	Stigler	End
Paul Mennett	Yale	End
Anderson	Sulphur	Tackle
Maurice Bill Giles	Bristow	Tackle
Thomas Edison Taylor	Sperry	Guard
Etheridge	Muskogee	Guard
Sprinkle	OC Classen	Center
Cecil Storm	Norman	Quarterback
Howard	Moore	Halfback
Charles DuBourdieu	Shattuck	Halfback
Byron Speaker	Cushing	Fullback

OKLAHOMA ALL-STATE FOOTBALL TEAM: 1934

FIRST TEAM

Name	School	Pos.	Ht.	Wt.	Age	Class
Ray Webba	OC Central	E	5-11	172	19	Senior
Alton Coppage	Hollis	E	6-1	170	19	Junior
Ralph Foster	Perry	T	6-0	195	18	Senior
Harry Juergens	Muskogee	T	6-1	195	18	Junior
Ralph Beaver	OC Capitol Hill	G	5-11	170	20	Senior
C. B. Coffey	Duncan	G	5-10	183	19	Senior
Vernon Mullens	Seminole	C	6-0	195	18	Senior
Gene Williams	Muskogee	QB	5-6	158	19	Senior
Orville Mathews	Chickasha	HB	5-8	168	20	Senior
Dave Egbert	Tulsa	HB	5-11	157	19	Junior
James Tyner	Sperry	FB	5-11	165	18	Senior
J. D. Norton	Weatherford	TB	5-9	160	18	Senior

SECOND TEAM

Name	School	Position
Smith	Stroud	End
Dan Perry	Tishomingo	End
R. M. Spradling	Texhoma	Tackle
Bonham	Jefferson	Tackle
Harris	Enid	Guard
Little	Kingfisher	Guard
Sieber	OC Classen	Center
Nathan Stufflebean	Pauls Valley	Quarterback
Watson	Idabel	Halfback
Floyd Johnston	Hennessey	Halfback
Don Short	McAlester	Fullback

THIRD TEAM

Erven Olson	Tulsa	End
Lee	Carman	End
Bill Reynolds	OC Capitol Hill	Tackle
Amos Goodfox	Pawnee	Tackle
Bradley	OC Central	Guard
Gowen	Broken Bow	Guard
Fred Bailey	Muskogee	Center
B. Checotah	Britton	Quarterback
Otis Rogers	Oilton	Halfback
George Farmer	Holdenville	Halfback
Troy Scholl	Eufaula	Fullback

OKLAHOMA ALL-STATE FOOTBALL TEAM: 1935

FIRST TEAM

Name	School	Pos.	Ht.	Wt.	Age	Class
Clifton Speegle	OC Capitol Hill	E	6-1	168	18	Senior
Lee Roy Beason	Snyder	E	6-2	170	18	Senior
Amos Goodfox	Pawnee	T	6-1	185	19	Senior
J. R. Manley	Hollis	T	6-1	193	18	Senior
Torrey Smith	Norman	G	5-11	168	18	Senior
Warren Ford	Blackwell	G	5-11	200	18	Senior
Wayne Hildreth	Fairview	C	6-2	190	18	Senior
Junius Plunkett	Wagoner	QB	5-10	165	17	Senior
Nathan Stufflebean	Pauls Valley	HB	6-0	180	19	Senior
Bruce Massey	Broken Bow	HB	5-10	150	18	Senior
Winfred W. Bynum	OC Central	FB	5-9	157	19	Senior

SECOND TEAM

Name	School	Position
Bill Jennings	Norman	End
Kenneth Sharp	Henryetta	End
Leo Sas	Bartlesville	Tackle
Gerlick	Yukon	Tackle
Jack Reynolds	Shawnee	Guard
Posey	Duncan	Guard
Blalock	Pauls Valley	Center
Dave Egbert	Tulsa	Quarterback
Russell Hyde	Waurika	Halfback
Carl Rivers	Kingfisher	Halfback
Bob Peoples	OC Classen	Fullback

THIRD TEAM

Perry	Purcell	End
Shirk	OC Central	End
Edgemon	Zaneis	Tackle
Teeter	Granfield	Tackle
William Haun	El Reno	Guard
Gene Crank	Muskogee	Guard
Caldwell	Durant	Center
Blevins	Greenfield	Quarterback
Chisholm	Haileyville	Halfback
Hopkins	Ringling	Halfback
Sharp	Wewoka	Fullback

OKLAHOMA ALL–STATE FOOTBALL TEAM: 1936

FIRST TEAM

Name	School	Pos.	Ht.	Wt.	Age	Class
Hoyt Decker	Henryetta	E	6-0	175	20	Senior
Lyle Smith	Fairview	E	6-2	183	17	Senior
George Dunlap	Pawhuska	T	5-9	190	19	Senior
Gene Hunt	Yale	T	6-0	255	19	Senior
Tommy Robertson	Duncan	G	6-1	190	19	Senior
Hercel Hickman	Stigler	G	6-1	190	19	Senior
Novel Wood	Norman	C	5-11	163	18	Senior
J. S. Munsey	Norman	B	5-11	153	19	Senior
Raymond Mallouf	Sayre	B	5-11	180	18	Senior
John Martin	Broken Bow	B	6-3	190	18	Senior
Bob Peoples	OC Classen	B	5-11	180	17	Senior

SECOND TEAM

Name	School	Position
Seiber	OC Classen	End
Kitchens	Purcell	End
Denzil Sparlin	Lawton	Tackle
Harold W. Lahar	OC Central	Tackle
Hughey	Wewoka	Guard
Delmer Haun	El Reno	Guard
Blalock	Pauls Valley	Center
Jack Jacobs	Muskogee	Back
Paul Woodson	OC Capital Hill	Back
Bill Jennings	Norman	Back
Elmer Lee Gentry	Shawnee	Back

THIRD TEAM

Name	School	Position
Al Hunter	Shawnee	End
Winters	Carnegie	End
Frank Stepp	OC Classen	Tackle
Teney Smith	Norman	Tackle
Cliff Trice	Waurika	Guard
K. Wolf	Miami	Guard
Williams	Wilson	Center
Glenn Gibson	Konawa	Back
Norman Robinson	Holdenville	Back
Montgomery	Britton	Back
Marvin Whitehead	Hollis	Back

OKLAHOMA ALL-STATE FOOTBALL TEAM: 1937

FIRST TEAM

Name	School	Pos.	Ht.	Wt.	Age	Class
Mack Creager	Tulsa	E	6-0	170	18	Junior
Merle Herman	Watonga	E	6-2	170	20	Senior
Roger Eason	OC Central	T	6-2	200	19	Senior
C. B. Stanley	Holdenville	T	6-4	207	18	Senior
Morris Haynie	Durant	G	6-1	195	18	Senior
John Thatcher	Stillwater	G	5-10	174	17	Senior
Don Witcraft	Fairfax	C	6-0	170	19	Senior
N. A. Keithley	Miami	B	5-10	160	18	Senior
Paul Woodson	OC Capitol Hill	B	6-0	213	19	Senior
Marvin Whitehead	Hollis	B	6-0	190	19	Senior
Jack Jacobs	Muskogee	B	6-1	185	18	Senior

SECOND TEAM

Name	School	Position
Joe Pounder	OC Classen	End
Cotton Benson	Frederick	End
Leon Cook	Enid	Tackle
Billy Van Edwards	Ponca City	Tackle
James Clancey	Pond Creek	Guard
Glenn Watson	Henryetta	Guard
F. C. Williams	Walters	Center
Damon Renfro	Pawhuska	Back
Tom Wheelus	Huge	Back
Jack Wurtz	Perry	Back
Phil Prigmore	Alva	Back

THIRD TEAM

Fred Jameson	Woodward	End
Gene McClary	Yale	End
Henry Darragh	Guthrie	Tackle
Harold Eiseman	Cleveland	Tackle
Marion Hutcheson	Sand Springs	Guard
Clark Harbert	Tishomingo	Guard
Dwight Weedn	Elk City	Center
Johnny Owens	Tipton	Back
Buddy Oster	Hobart	Back
Buck Wray	Yukon	Back
Sam Kolman	Purcell	Back

OKLAHOMA ALL-STATE FOOTBALL TEAM: 1938

NORTH

Ends

Name	Height	Weight	School
J. T. Recer	6-0	170	Perkins
Buck Henderson	5-11	186	Ponca City
Vergil Craig	6-2	175	Hennessey
Hubert Callaway	5-10	165	Muskogee

Tackles

Jim Hughey	6-2	185	Cherokee
Tommy Tallchief	6-3	205	Fairfax
Frank Kirkpatrick	6-1	200	Blackwell
Meredith Hutchinson	6-2	237	Sand Springs

Guards

Dick Palmer	6-0	185	OC Classen
Grant Helton	5-9	162	Miami
Edward McCain	5-11	175	Okmulgee
Leon McKenzie	5-9	176	Guthrie

Centers

Frank Capps	6-0	188	Pawhuska
Jack Steck	6-1	195	Sapulpa

Backs

Phil Prigmore	5-11	165	Alva
J. C. Meek	5-10	170	Chandler
Joe Pounder	6-0	190	OC Classen
Carl Burget	5-8	165	Dewey
Dene Harp	6-0	178	Fairview
Olin Miller	5-9	160	Stillwater
Lindell Hays	5-10	175	Wagoner
Wonk Abel	5-10	170	Tulsa Webster

OKLAHOMA ALL-STATE FOOTBALL TEAM: 1938

SOUTH

Ends

Name	Height	Weight	School
W. G. Lamb	6-0	175	Ardmore
Ervin Oesterie	6-3	193	Henryetta
Ancil Young	6-2	170	Norman
Ralph Schilling	6-2	175	Seminole

Tackles

W. B. Mayfield	6-3	205	Carnegie
Buel McDowell	6-4	235	Hugo
Rollo Clifford	6-2	215	Wewoka
Arlo Lund	6-2	185	Lawton

Guards

Laddie Birge	6-2	215	Duncan
J. L. Cloyd	5-10	170	McAlester
Sammy Stevens	5-11	189	Walters
Albert Gregory	6-0	185	Okemah

Centers

Tommy Moulton	6-0	175	OC Capitol Hill
Vernon Newell	6-0	175	Shawnee

Backs

Harold Slape	5-10	160	Altus
Dee Harrison	5-11	185	Bowlegs
Altus Avery	5-11	175	OC Capitol Hill
Huel Hamm	6-1	180	OC Central
Roy Cagle	6-0	180	OC Central
Perry Seddon	5-11	176	Hollis
Dick Mercer	5-9	150	Ada
Glenn Dobbs	6-2	182	Frederick

OKLAHOMA ALL-STATE FOOTBALL TEAM: 1939

NORTH

Ends

Name	Height	Weight	School
Kenneth Spence	6-0	170	Pawhuska
Donald McDonald	6-3	194	Commerce
Jack Nash	6-1	175	Drumright
Quinton Poe	6-1	175	Miami

Tackles

Jack Jordon	6-1	210	Garber
Richard Boepple	5-11	188	Enid
Eli Pricer	6-0	185	Perry
J. D. Cheek	6-1	210	Stillwater

Guards

Lawrence Labarthe	6-1	196	Tonkawa
Harvey Stone	5-11	190	Cushing
Mannie Wiley	5-10	175	Sapulpa
Warren Witt	6-0	165	Ponca City

Centers

Wayne Adams	6-0	190	Hominy
Bob Thomas	5-11	180	Okmulgee

Backs

Jack Marguette	5-10	170	OC Classen
Tate Hale	6-0	210	Okmulgee
Weldon Hambrick	5-11	185	OC Northeast
Lee Cook	6-0	170	OC Classen
Eddie Davis	6-1	170	Muskogee
Clinton Cranmer	5-11	150	Bartlesville
Ted Brunt	5-10	180	Pawhuska
Frank Scott	5-11	176	Okeene

OKLAHOMA ALL-STATE FOOTBALL TEAM: 1939

SOUTH

Ends

Name	Height	Weight	School
Dave Richeson	6-0	170	Shawnee
Lester Hill	6-1	190	Walters
Jim Tyree	6-2	190	OC Capitol Hill
Grady McGee	5-11	175	Altus

Tackles

Max Moore	6-0	205	Durant
Kenneth Hightower	6-0	210	Duncan
Grover Marshall	6-0	190	Henryetta
R. Kane	6-1	200	Ada

Guards

Johnny M. Johnson	5-10	180	Elk City
Joe Jones	6-0	195	Wewoka
Pete Tillman	6-0	185	Mangum
Vernon Purcell	5-7	150	Lawton

Centers

Max Fischer	6-3	178	Norman
Bill LeGrange	6-1	175	OC Central

Backs

Lloyd Stephens	6-0	185	Ada
Bob Cunningham	6-0	180	Hollis
Frank Dunson	5-10	160	Wewoka
George Boudreau	6-1	185	Purcell
Ed Jeffres	6-3	195	McAlester
Bill Bellamy	5-11	175	OC Central
Junior Golding	6-1	180	Eufaula
Carl Brewington	6-0	179	Shawnee

OKLAHOMA ALL-STATE FOOTBALL TEAM: 1940

NORTH

Ends

Name	Age	Ht.	Wt.	School
James Tebow	17	5-11	165	Enid
Archie Bradley	16	6-0	174	Muskogee
Louis Hayes	19	6-1	160	Tulsa Webster
Gordon McDowell	17	6-2	170	Cherokee

Tackles

J. R. Hill	18	5-11	185	Okmulgee
James Ward	17	6-2	180	Shattuck
Vaughn Shirley	18	6-3	194	OC Classen
Dwight Deming	18	6-2	185	Weatherford

Guards

Jack Lairmore	17	5-11	185	Tulsa Central
Buddy Courtney	19	5-11	171	Medford
Adrian Paul	18	6-0	175	Fairview
Ben Stout	17	6-0	190	OC Classen

Centers

Bob Beames	19	6-2	180	Tonkawa
Otis Schellstede	19	6-2	185	Blackwell

Backs

Dudley Carson	16	5-8	140	Muskogee
Clyde LeForce	17	5-11	165	Bristow
Kirby Rider	19	5-11	175	Ponca City
Elmer Simmons	16	5-8	137	Enid
Hollis Copeland	19	5-11	185	Tulsa Central
Harvey McKibben	18	6-4	222	Miami
Wheeler Gayton	19	6-0	175	Hominy
Raymond Morris	19	6-1	185	Britton

OKLAHOMA ALL-STATE FOOTBALL TEAM: 1940

SOUTH

Ends

Name	Age	Ht.	Wt.	School
Billy Houck	17	5-11	170	Mangum
Buddy Goodall	17	6-2	190	Ada
O'Quinn Dunn	18	6-2	195	Chickasha
Warren Childers	17	6-1	175	Frederick

Tackles

Nelson Greene	18	6-2	190	Shawnee
Harold Simeroth	19	6-4	210	Purcell
Frank Thompson	19	6-2	195	Moore
Albert Downs	19	6-2	197	Atoka

Guards

Charles Floyd	19	5-11	175	McAlester
C. F. Bryce	18	5-10	194	Altus
Elmer Duncan	18	6-0	185	Seminole
Cleon Rhodes	20	5-9	170	Mountain View

Centers

LeRoy Garren	18	6-0	190	Maud
Bud O'Dea	18	6-1	185	Durant

Backs

J. C. Byrd	18	5-10	160	Lawton
Joe Bill Whisenant	18	5-10	178	Duncan
Darrell Harris	17	5-11	177	Madill
Son Riley	19	6-0	180	OC Capitol Hill
Don Fauble	16	6-1	170	Shawnee
Warren Trent	17	5-9	165	Prague
Clinton Carr	18	5-8	165	Marlow
Oscar Raglin	19	5-8	162	OC Central

OKLAHOMA ALL-STATE FOOTBALL TEAM: 1941

NORTH

Ends

Name	School	Age	Ht.	Wt.	Coach
Bill Short	Alva	18	6-2	190	Dean Simon
John Cooper	Drumright	19	6-0	180	Buck Weaver
Dorman Morsman	Kingfisher	17	6-1	185	Pete Rivers
Fred Hurst	Chandler	18	6-1	178	Red Barnes

Tackles

Name	School	Age	Ht.	Wt.	Coach
Homer Paine	Enid	17	6-1	200	Wallace Lawson
Quinton Schafer	Fairfax	17	6-0	195	Ross Case
Buddy Burris	Muskogee	18	5-11	190	Paul Marston
Charles Graybill	Nowata	18	5-11	185	B. Bombgardner

Guards

Name	School	Age	Ht.	Wt.	Coach
Tony Lyons	OC Classen	17	6-3	170	Leo Higbie
Clyde Kimes	Perry	20	6-2	185	Hump Daniels
Warren Edwards	Ponca City	18	5-9	155	Earl Sullins
Dick Bland	Tulsa Rogers	17	6-2	180	Leo Howard

Centers

Name	School	Age	Ht.	Wt.	Coach
Gordon Silvey	Henryetta	17	6-0	185	Marion Anglin
Jack Taylor	Shattuck	18	6-1	168	Ira Littlejohn

Backs

Name	School	Age	Ht.	Wt.	Coach
Merlin London	Blackwell	17	6-1	168	W. M. Ledbetter
Derald Lebow	Okmulgee	17	5-11	170	Eddie Brady
Ray Ary	OC Northeast	19	6-1	180	H. McManus
Walley Spencer	Tonkawa	18	5-11	155	Harold Piper
Paul Annex	Tulsa Central	18	5-6	130	Melvin Riggs
Earl Perry	Tulsa Webster	17	5-9	152	Marshall Minton
Owen Roof	Thomas	18	6-2	180	Charles J. Ross
Howard Spoon	Picher	17	5-8	158	Claud Pierce

OKLAHOMA ALL-STATE FOOTBALL TEAM: 1941

SOUTH

Ends

Name	School	Age	Ht.	Wt.	Coach
James Wilson	Seminole	17	6-4	180	Gene Corrotto
Willie Ellis	Shawnee	19	5-11	160	Ray LeCrone
Ralph Jennings	Carnegie	17	6-1	180	Sivil Pickett
Jake Lucas	Weleetka	17	6-0	185	Butch McKinney

Tackles

Delton Marcum	Ada	18	5-11	185	Klvan George
J. B. Hammons	Lone Wolf	16	5-11	212	J. W. Steele
T. D. Beavers	Marlow	19	5-11	205	S. Spradlling
Bob Sanders	Chickasha	16	6-0	195	J. Williamson

Guards

Bill Landers	Pauls Valley	18	5-11	165	Ray Thompson
Bill Hickman	Duncan	18	5-11	195	Billy Stamps
Jerry Greasby	Mangum	18	5-11	162	Weldon Spivey
Sam Allison	Wewoka	18	6-1	165	Cliff Speegle

Centers

Jean Fitter	Altus	17	6-0	170	Johnny Gregg
Joe Louis Resneder	Hobart	17	6-0	170	Ken Gallagher

Backs

Wendell Sullivan	Lawton	18	6-0	175	Glenn Dosser
LeRoy Esadooah	Lawton	18	5-11	155	Glenn Dosser
Otis McCary	Atoka	17	6-0	188	Lester Secrest
J. T. Williams	Durant	19	5-11	175	Jack Byrom
Bob Berry	Norman	18	6-0	160	Chalky Stogner
Phil Cluck	Bowlegs	18	5-10	170	Vernon Mullen
Warren Wood	Ardmore	18	5-11	160	Paul Young
Lloyd White	Walters	17	6-2	195	J. D. Norton

OKLAHOMA ALL-STATE FOOTBALL TEAM: 1942

NORTH

Ends

Name	Age	Ht.	Wt.	School	Class
Lewis Dunn	18	5-11	180	Nowata	Senior
Curtis Harris	18	6-1	185	OC Classen	Senior
Robert Askey	17	5-10	170	Ponca City	Senior
Jim LaRue	17	5-11	165	Clinton	Senior

Tackles

Name	Age	Ht.	Wt.	School	Class
Millard Cummings	18	6-1	185	Enid	Senior
James Kolb	17	6-4	215	Pawnee	Senior
Leon Simmons	18	6-1	172	Enid	Senior
Pat McLarty	17	5-11	180	Okmulgee	Senior

Guards

Name	Age	Ht.	Wt.	School	Class
Merle Casford	17	5-10	170	Tonkawa	Senior
Paul Thomas	18	6-1	202	Pawnee	Senior
Tom Cox	18	5-10	165	Hominy	Senior
Walter Stevenson	17	5-11	160	Medford	Senior

Centers

Name	Age	Ht.	Wt.	School	Class
John St. Clair	17	5-9	165	Perry	Senior
Cleaborn O'Kelly	17	6-2	170	Tulsa Central	Senior

Quarterbacks

Name	Age	Ht.	Wt.	School	Class
Warren Nichols	16	6-2	185	Watonga	Senior
Lewis Maxwell	18	5-11	155	Tulsa Webster	Senior

Halfbacks

Name	Age	Ht.	Wt.	School	Class
Bennie Ballard	18	6-0	175	Nowata	Senior
James Leierer	18	6-2	188	Enid	Senior
J. D. Roland	17	6-0	180	El Reno	Senior
Kenneth Roof	17	5-10	168	Thomas	Senior

Fullbacks

Name	Age	Ht.	Wt.	School	Class
Bob Fenimore	17	6-1	183	Woodward	Senior
Bill Baldwin	18	6-0	195	Tulsa Rogers	Senior

OKLAHOMA ALL-STATE FOOTBALL TEAM: 1942

SOUTH

Ends

Name Age	Age	Ht.	Wt.	School	Class
Thomas Reynolds	20	6-2	175	Madill	Senior
G. W. Pool	18	5-10	160	Bowlegs	Senior
Gerald Harp	18	6-1	190	Shawnee	Senior
Jerry Bailes	16	6-1	188	Stigler	Senior

Tackles

Norman McNabb	18	5-11	195	Norman	Senior
James Gassaway	17	6-1	220	Poteau	Senior
Joe Bishop	17	5-10	175	Hobart	Senior
Richard Carpenter	17	5-9	175	OC Capitol Hill	Senior

Guards

Melvin Brookey	17	5-10	185	Henryetta	Senior
Cecil Sumpter	17	5-11	192	Hollis	Senior
Harold Latham	17	5-10	167	Chickasha	Senior
Vernon Parlier	18	5-7	150	Ardmore	Senior

Centers

Leon Files	17	5-11	187	Henryetta	Senior
Buford Pringle	19	6-1	200	Lawton	Senior

Quarterbacks

Darrell Royal	18	5-11	165	Hollis	Senior
George Dunlap	17	5-11	165	Wilburton	Senior

Halfbacks

Billy Tucker	17	5-11	164	Ringling	Senior
Wayne Burd	18	5-9	175	Holdenville	Senior
Audie Derryberry	20	5-10	175	Altus	Senior
Louis Dollarhide	19	6-1	175	Idabel	Senior

Fullbacks

Bill Jordan	19	6-0	180	OC Central	Senior
Howard Hawkins	18	6-2	195	Purcell	Senior

OKLAHOMA ALL-STATE FOOTBALL TEAM: 1943

NORTH

Ends

Name	Age	Ht.	Wt.	School	Class
Stanley West	18	6-0	190	Enid	Senior
William Taylor	17	6-0	180	Vinita	Senior
Tom Cordell	17	6-3	195	Bartlesville	Senior
Richard Moseley	16	5-11	170	Muskogee	Senior

Tackles

Doyle Monger	17	6-0	220	Pawhuska	Senior
Carl Harris	18	5-8	238	Stroud	Senior
William Kongable	17	6-1	175	Hominy	Senior
Leon Thornton	17	6-0	190	Prague	Senior

Guards

James Arnold	18	5-9	160	Tulsa Webster	Senior
Donald Mertz	17	5-11	170	Ponca City	Senior
Hubert Forney	18	5-10	175	Perry	Senior
Walter Schmidt	16	5-11	187	Miami	Senior

Centers

J. Frank Howard	16	6-0	170	Cushing	Senior
William Arnold	16	5-11	170	Guthrie	Senior

Backs

Basil Sharpe	17	6-0	185	Pawnee	Senior
Bobby Jack Stuart	17	5-11	180	Tulsa Rogers	Senior
Perry Moss	17	5-9	150	Tulsa Central	Senior
Jack Dodd	18	5-10	175	Tulsa Webster	Senior
Leonard Dunn	18	5-11	165	Nowata	Senior
Jack Harp	17	6-0	180	Fairview	Senior
Lavern Williams	17	5-11	175	Deer Creek	Senior
Carl Stephens	17	6-0	170	OC Classen	Senior

OKLAHOMA ALL-STATE FOOTBALL TEAM: 1943

SOUTH

Ends

Name	Age	Ht.	Wt.	School	Class
Raymond Barry	17	6-2	185	Hollis	Senior
Paul Graham	18	6-0	195	Shawnee	Senior
John Scott	18	6-1	170	Norman	Senior
Ralph Oliphant	18	6-2	180	Holdenville	Senior

Tackles

Name	Age	Ht.	Wt.	School	Class
Gene Bradney	18	5-10	240	Henryetta	Senior
Bill Waters	18	6-4	210	OC Capitol Hill	Senior
Leonard Chapman	18	6-0	200	Altus	Senior
Bob Logan	16	5-11	178	Poteau	Senior

Guards

Name	Age	Ht.	Wt.	School	Class
L. P. Brown	18	5-11	155	Duncan	Senior
Calvin Price	17	5-10	155	Norman	Senior
Mickey McCarty	17	5-8	175	Maud	Senior
Joe Cooksey	17	5-7	175	Pauls Valley	Senior

Centers

Name	Age	Ht.	Wt.	School	Class
Pat Dunn	18	6-0	165	Healdton	Senior
P. L. Wheeler	17	6-1	170	Clinton	Senior

Backs

Name	Age	Ht.	Wt.	School	Class
Douglas Nix	17	5-10	160	Duncan	Senior
J. R. Eddy	18	5-11	180	Davis	Senior
Tom Meason	18	5-11	180	Ardmore	Senior
Charles Piatt	18	6-0	192	Yukon	Senior
Robert Williams	17	5-11	170	Weatherford	Senior
Pete Warren	17	6-0	165	Lawton	Senior
Johnny Juett	17	5-11	165	Durant	Senior
Jimmy Farmer	16	6-0	185	Mangum	Senior

OKLAHOMA ALL-STATE FOOTBALL TEAM: 1944

NORTH

Ends

Name	Age	Ht.	Wt.	School	Class
Paul Lewis	17	6-0	174	Bristow	Senior
Bill Long	17	6-2	187	Hominy	Senior
Jim Owens	18	6-3	186	OC Classen	Senior
Johnny Walker	17	5-11	163	Tulsa Central	Senior

Tackles

Bob Greggs	17	6-1	189	Pawhuska	Senior
George Hall	17	6-0	197	Perry	Senior
Eugene Hinton	17	6-2	231	Drumright	Senior
Jim Storts	18	6-1	198	Tulsa Rogers	Senior

Guards

Bob Dauber	17	5-11	176	Woodward	Senior
Orville Hare	17	6-0	186	Sand Springs	Senior
Charles Shaw	17	6-1	184	OC Classen	Senior
Robert Silvy	17	5-9	179	Ponca City	Senior

Centers

A. J. Ingram	17	5-11	176	Davenport	Senior
George Keck	17	6-2	177	Fairview	Senior

Backs

Gordon Beville	17	6-0	178	Vinta	Senior
Sam Bratcher	17	5-9	173	Claremore	Senior
John Carey	17	5-11	159	Guthrie	Senior
Stanley Gwinn	17	5-8	153	Tulsa Central	Senior
Leo Kitterman	18	5-10	169	Garber	Senior
Jack Meier	17	6-1	184	Commerce	Senior
Alfred Needs	18	6-1	191	El Reno	Senior
Carl Ropp	18	5-9	158	Dewey	Senior

OKLAHOMA ALL-STATE FOOTBALL TEAM: 1944

SOUTH

Ends

Name	Age	Ht.	Wt.	School	Class
Robert Brown	17	6-0	178	Frederick	Senior
Kenneth Jones	17	6-0	168	Wewoka	Senior
Don Van Pool	17	6-2	191	OC Capitol Hill	Senior
Wesley Virden	17	5-11	169	Stigler	Senior

Tackles

Robert Bauman	17	5-11	182	Altus	Senior
Bob Faucett	17	6-0	181	Shawnee	Senior
Eugene McDaniels	17	6-2	193	Wetumka	Senior
Bill Simeroth	17	6-0	195	Purcell	Senior

Guards

Harmon Crawford	17	5-10	167	Ardmore	Senior
Bob Ensley	17	5-11	172	Lawton	Senior
Tommy Nelson	18	6-1	193	Mangum	Senior
Leo Shipley	17	5-10	169	Chickasha	Senior

Centers

Bob Bodenhamer	17	6-2	192	Waurika	Senior
Boyd McGugan	17	6-0	163	Holdenville	Senior

Backs

Bill Ayres	17	5-11	175	Madill	Senior
Bill Boswell	18	6-0	212	Maud	Senior
Jack Fenton	17	5-7	146	Ada	Senior
Bill Grimes	18	6-0	179	Comanche	Senior
Leslie Ming	18	5-11	187	OC Central	Senior
Bill Remy	18	5-10	162	Norman	Senior
Preston Robertson	17	5-10	164	Poteau	Senior
Arthur Stewart	18	5-10	172	Wilson	Senior

OKLAHOMA ALL-STATE FOOTBALL TEAM: 1945

NORTH

Ends

Name	Wt.	Ht.	Age	School	Class
Eldon Janzen	189	6-4	17	Medford	Senior
Jack Shelton	197	6-6	17	Stillwater	Senior
James Griffin	173	6-2	18	Putnam City	Senior
Joe Crowder	187	6-4	17	Muskogee	Senior

Tackles

Bill Garner	181	5-11	18	Tulsa Rogers	Senior
Jack Hyer	221	6-2	17	Woodward	Senior
James Miller	191	6-0	17	Guthrie	Senior
Max Druen	187	6-2	17	Enid	Senior

Guards

Frankie Anderson	184	6-0	17	OC Northeast	Senior
George McKean	169	5-9	17	OC Classen	Senior
Jim Gregson	181	5-11	17	Blackwell	Senior
James Ussery	169	5-11	18	Tulsa Webster	Senior

Centers

James Hendren	172	5-10	17	Pryor	Senior
Charles Dowell	186	6-1	17	Tulsa Central	Senior

Backs

Wilson Wagner	187	6-1	17	Nowata	Senior
Bob Ford	168	5-10	17	Bristow	Senior
James Coventon	183	5-11	16	Wagoner	Senior
Louis Rybka	161	5-10	17	Dewey	Senior
Dennis Rountree	180	5-11	17	Fairview	Senior
Stacy Howell	162	6-2	17	Pawnee	Senior
Marvin Bohannon	168	5-10	17	Perry	Senior
Ronald Dry	209	6-2	17	Fairland	Senior

OKLAHOMA ALL-STATE FOOTBALL TEAM: 1945

SOUTH

Ends

Name	Wt.	Ht.	Age	School	Class
Waldo Schaaf	193	6-0	17	Chickasha	Senior
Bob Eubank	179	6-0	17	Norman	Senior
LeRoy Montgomery	184	6-2	17	Lawton	Senior
Cecil Fassio	172	6-1	18	Wilburton	Senior

Tackles

Name	Wt.	Ht.	Age	School	Class
Bennie Davis	219	6-1	17	McAlester	Senior
Richard Simmons	269	6-8	19	Seminole	Senior
Kenneth Fogelsong	209	5-11	17	Anadarko	Senior
E. G. Stewart	187	6-1	17	OC Capitol Hill	Senior

Guards

Name	Wt.	Ht.	Age	School	Class
Melrose Minton	183	5-11	17	Sayre	Senior
James Harris	186	6-0	17	Duncan	Senior
Don Presley	197	5-11	17	Ada	Senior
Billy Farley	182	5-10	17	Altus	Senior

Centers

Name	Wt.	Ht.	Age	School	Class
Bill Ashby	181	6-0	16	Shawnee	Senior
W. C. Martin	179	6-1	17	Mangum	Senior

Backs

Name	Wt.	Ht.	Age	School	Class
Clifford Van Meter	194	6-0	18	Henryetta	Senior
Hooter Brewer	171	6-0	17	Pauls Valley	Senior
Frank Boydston	181	5-11	17	OC Central	Senior
Sid Beames	176	6-0	17	Tishomingo	Senior
Duane Bates	179	5-11	17	Clinton	Senior
Pat Cashman	142	5-7	17	Ardmore	Senior
Jimmy Thomason	156	5-9	17	Holdenville	Senior
Bill Lambeth	182	6-3	17	Maud	Senior

OKLAHOMA ALL-STATE FOOTBALL TEAM: 1946

NORTH

Ends

Name	School	Age	Ht.	Wt.	Coach
Billy Glenn	Putnam City	19	6-2	181	Mutt Herring
John Hooker	Dewey	17	6-1	183	L. D. Bash
Dwight Huffman	Medford	19	6-0	191	Howard Welborn
Dick Stratten	Commerce	17	6-4	186	Allen Woolard

Tackles

John Bilyeu	Pawhuska	20	6-3	228	Frank Lucas
Richard Doak	Bristow	18	6-2	208	Mose LeForce
Joe Horkey	Tulsa Central	17	6-1	203	Melvin Riggs
Bennie Reaves	OC Northeast	18	5-11	188	Hack McManus

Guards

Danny Blubaugh	Tonkawa	17	5-10	170	Buck Butcher
Jack Bolinger	Tulsa Rogers	18	5-11	174	Lieb Richmond
Albert Prado	Ponca City	17	6-1	208	Earl Sullins
Don Riederer	Sapulpa	17	5-8	194	B. Bombardner

Centers

Richard Jones.	Drumright	17	5-10	172	Olin H. Wilson
Gerald Lyon	Alva	17	6-2	188	Dean Simon

Backs

Bill Brown	Bartlesville	17	5-11	182	Lennie E. Adams
Ed Dooley	OC Classen	18	5-8	162	Leo K. Higbie
Henry Frnka, Jr.	Tulsa Rogers	17	5-11	168	Lieb Richmond
Bob Gillaspy	Chandler	17	6-2	170	Tip Jacobson
Kenneth Jacks	Pryor	17	5-10	181	Howard Hunsaker
J. D. Maggard	Nowata	18	5-11	184	George McCoy
Jack Shawgo	Tulsa Central	18	6-1	205	Melvin Riggs
Bob Wheat	Fairview	17	5-11	182	George Eubanks
Floyd Winfield	Enid	20	5-9	171	Wallace Lawson

OKLAHOMA ALL-STATE FOOTBALL TEAM: 1946

SOUTH

Ends

Name	School	Age	Ht.	Wt.	Coach
Jimmy Acree	Maud	18	6-3	195	George Tallchief
Arden McDaniels	Chickasha	17	6-3	182	Vern Harris
Duane Prince	OC Capitol Hill	17	6-2	174	G. Miskovsky
Billy Paul Thomason	Altus	20	6-0	185	Hal Hilpirt

Tackles

Name	School	Age	Ht.	Wt.	Coach
Bill Allen	Idabel	20	6-3	219	Woody Holman
J. D. Cole	Hollis	19	6-1	189	Joe B. Metcalf
Laddie McDade	Duncan	18	6-2	208	Billy Stamps
Bill Miner	Checotah	17	6-2	209	Roy Gardner

Guards

Name	School	Age	Ht.	Wt.	Coach
Charles Dyer	Marlow	17	5-10	171	L. L. Teakell
James Huddleston	Poteau	18	5-11	170	Burl Stidham
Kenneth Ingraham	OC Central	17	6-0	182	Olen Williams
Calvin Myers	Lawton	18	5-11	198	Glenn Dosser

Centers

Name	School	Age	Ht.	Wt.	Coach
Benny Ashby	Shawnee	16	6-0	184	Ray LeCrene
Reece McGee	Norman	18	6-1	192	Doc LaFevers

Backs

Name	School	Age	Ht.	Wt.	Coach
Vernon Brewer	Sayre	18	5-8	182	Homer Tanner
Joe Cunningham	Purcell	18	6-0	172	Boney Mathews
Tommy Gray	Seminole	17	5-11	149	Gene Corrotto
Dick Heathley	Mangum	19	5-11	174	Earl R. Presley
Al Lens	Lawton	19	6-2	189	Glenn Dosser
Lindell Pearson	OC Capitol Hill	17	6-1	184	John Miskovsky
Gene Read	Ardmore	17	5-9	168	Paul Young
Robert Shipman	Okemah	17	6-0	180	Wayne Prichard

OKLAHOMA ALL-STATE FOOTBALL TEAM: 1947

NORTH

Ends

Name	School	Age	Ht.	Wt.	Coach
Bill Beckman	Muskogee	17	6-0	183	Paul Young
Tom Dark	Broken Arrow	17	6-2	181	Herman Ragsdale
Eddie Roberts	Pawnee	16	6-4	196	O. C. Cearley
Louie Surber	Pawhuska	17	5-11	171	Frank Lucas

Tackles

Bob Collins	Tulsa Central	18	6-0	198	Melvin Riggs
Bud Crutchfield	Bristow	20	6-0	219	Mose LeForce
Jerry Stubbs	Stillwater	17	6-0	201	Ralph Hamilton
John Wakley	Tulsa Webster	17	5-11	194	Leslie Van Noy

Guards

Tommy Alexander	Pryer	17	6-0	189	H. Hunsaker
Robert Claibourn	Dewey	17	5-9	178	L. D. Bash
Bob Wittich	Guthrie	17	5-11	173	Lyle Yarbrough
Lester Wright	OC Northeast	18	5-7	174	Hack McManus

Centers

Guy Fuller	OC Classen	17	6-1	203	Jim Conger
Lonnie Keck	Fairview	17	5-11	174	George Eubanks

Backs

Bill Breedlove	Vinita	17	5-10	172	Bob Thomas
Jack Culley	El Reno	17	5-10	173	Jenks Simmons
L. D. Leedy	Weatherford	17	6-2	192	Steve Graham
Bill Lonebear	Thomas	20	6-0	184	Joe Ross
Dick McCaffree	Cherokee	17	6-0	185	Earl Crowder
John Mueller	Okmulgee	17	6-1	182	Ed Brady
Dick Powell	Ponca City	17	5-10	169	Earl Sullins
Leon Sandel	Tulsa Rogers	17	5-9	156	Lieb Richmond

OKLAHOMA ALL-STATE FOOTBALL TEAM: 1947

SOUTH

Ends

Name	School	Age	Ht.	Wt.	Coach
Don Broyles	Hugo	18	6-0	179	Simon Parker
Ed Gipson	OC Central	18	6-1	181	Olen Williams
Don Johnson	Chickasha	18	6-3	192	Vern Harris
Bennie Leonard	Henryetta	17	6-1	173	Marion Anglin

Tackles

Name	School	Age	Ht.	Wt.	Coach
Richard Eddy	Checotah	17	6-1	214	Bogner Stubbs
Bob Faulkner	Idabel	16	6-0	196	Woody Holman
J. N. Johnson	Norman	19	6-1	186	Doc Lefevers
Leroy Marshall	OC Capitol Hill	20	6-1	198	John Miskovsky

Guards

Name	School	Age	Ht.	Wt.	Coach
Oral Peak	Sulphur	18	6-0	188	Jack Cox
Ted Rupe	Wewoka	18	5-10	195	Paul Greene
Ray Smith	Duncan	18	5-9	164	John Davenport
Raymond Urbrazo	Anadarko	17	5-11	196	Smitty Williams

Centers

Name	School	Age	Ht.	Wt.	Coach
Bob Griffin	Frederick	18	6-2	208	Earl Presley
Tommy Littrell	Holdenville	17	6-1	189	John Dougherty

Backs

Name	School	Age	Ht.	Wt.	Coach
David Branstetter	OC Central	17	5-10	171	Olen Williams
Scott Cummings	Elk City	17	5-9	165	George Scott
Charles Montgomery	Pauls Valley	18	5-10	146	Otis Delaporte
Glenn Oliver	Seminole	17	5-10	169	Gene Corrotto
Jime Rinehart	Frederick	18	5-11	178	Earl Presley
Willie Seddon	Hollis	18	5-11	156	Joe B. Metcalf
Frank Silva	Crooked Oak	17	5-11	179	Choctaw Smith
Chick Tiger	Altus	17	6-0	181	Hal Hilpirt

OKLAHOMA ALL-STATE FOOTBALL TEAM: 1948

NORTH

Ends

Name	School	Age	Ht.	Wt.	Coach
Lawrence Howard	Miami	18	5-11	167	George McCoy
Jennings Nelson	Enid	17	6-1	178	Ed Brady
Mo Odell	Watonga	16	6-1	185	Dean Wile
Phil Seagrove	Tulsa Rogers	17	6-0	169	Lieb Richmond

Tackles

Eugene Ball	Muskogee	18	6-0	183	Paul Young
Ernest Caten	Cushing	17	5-8	186	Melvin Skelton
James Holder	OC Northeast	17	6-0	218	Hack McManus
Carlton Wright	Sand Springs	17	6-2	198	Maurice Hall

Guards

Chet Bynum	OC Classen	17	5-11	184	Jim Conger
W. D. Goins	Vinita	19	5-11	201	Bob Thomas
Ray McNaught	Fairview	17	5-10	191	George Eubanks
John Weinmaster	Okeene	17	5-11	178	Oliver Webber

Centers

Tom Catlin	Ponca City	17	6-0	171	Earl Sullins
Howard Moss	Tulsa Central	17	6-0	182	Melvin Riggs

Backs

Dale Crawford	El Reno	18	5-11	167	Jenks Simmons
Eddie Crowder	Muskogee	17	6-1	152	Paul Young
Bud Godsoe	Chandler	17	6-2	205	Shelby Wyatt
Tom Hudspeth	Afton	17	5-11	158	Gene Wolf
Glen Hurd	Wagoner	17	6-0	173	A. M. Calloway
Paul King	Bristow	17	5-11	174	Mose LeForce
Billy Vessels	Cleveland	17	6-1	178	Lyle Berryhill
Harold West	Tulsa Webster	17	5-10	156	Leslie Van Noy

OKLAHOMA ALL-STATE FOOTBALL TEAM: 1948

SOUTH

Ends

Name	School	Age	Ht.	Wt.	Coach
Kenneth Cannady	Ryan	17	6-3	191	Jack Riddle
Bill Coffman	Holdenville	17	6-4	204	Jake Dougherty
James Pack	Duncan	20	6-0	181	John Davenport
Corliss Woods	Purcell	19	5-11	172	Beney Matthews

Tackles

Jerry Greasey	Chickasha	19	6-2	214	Joe Gibson
Raymon Herd	Grandfield	20	6-0	187	Cleodua Beavers
Eddie Wilburn	Wynnewood	17	6-1	226	Tex Bartlett
Delphens Winkleman	Lawton	20	5-10	188	Glenn Dosser

Guards

Bill Caudill	Altus	17	5-10	176	Hal Hilpirt
Bob Gilbert	Sayre	18	6-0	201	J. T. Adams
Ronald Paschal	Ardmore	17	5-11	178	George Holleway
Buster Smith	Waurika	20	5-11	183	Burl Thompson

Centers

Tom Heathcock	Seminole	19	6-1	178	Gene Corrotto
Bill Sirkel	OC Central	18	6-0	184	Antone Jacobson

Backs

Earlie Bynum	Hollis	20	5-11	177	Joe B. Medcalf
Tom Carroll	Okemah	16	6-0	172	Wayne Prichett
Gene Cook	Wewoka	18	5-10	186	Paul Greene
Bill Doty	Wilson	17	6-1	196	Aaron Dry
Bill Fox	Norman	16	6-1	176	Doc LeFevers
Merrill Green	Chickasha	19	5-9	168	Joe Gibson
Jim Pollock	OC Capitol Hill	17	5-8	166	John Miskovsky
Don Summers	Ada	18	6-0	202	Elvan George

OKLAHOMA ALL-STATE FOOTBALL TEAM: 1949

NORTH

Ends

Name	School	Age	Ht.	Wt.	Coach
George Elliott	Muskogee	17	6-0	171	Paul Young
Haskell Graves	OC Classen	18	6-0	179	Jim Conger
Tom Miner	Checotah	18	6-3	204	Bogner Stubbs
Jack Wear	Ponca City	19	6-0	172	Earl Sullins

Tackles

Ross Ausburn	Tulsa Rogers	18	6-0	196	Harry Knapp
George Cink	Medford	18	6-3	201	Howard Welborn
Bob Edwards	Stroud	18	6-1	205	Blue Gaither
Kenneth Frisbie	Picher	17	6-1	202	John R. Adams

Guards

Isaac McGrew	Okmulgee	19	5-9	191	Vern Harris
Don Page	Bartlesville	17	5-11	183	Burl Stidham
Gene Price	OC Northeast	18	5-8	173	Hack McManus
Kenneth Willits	Putnam City	17	5-10	172	Jim Reynolds

Centers

Gayle Davis	Shidler	18	5-11	196	Art Fleak
Kenneth Madewell	Sand Springs	18	6-6	221	Maurice Hall

Backs

Billy Bledsoe	Cushing	19	5-10	162	Melvin Skelton
Leo Canaday	Blackwell	18	6-0	174	Jack Mitchell
Jerry Goody	Tulsa Central	18	5-11	161	Melvin Riggs
Jack Ging	Alva	17	5-10	144	Dean Simon
Kenneth Lawson	Vinita	18	6-2	191	Bob Thomas
Fred Meyers	Enid	17	6-0	178	Ed Brady
Kenneth Sample	Miami	17	5-10	166	George McCoy
Bill Walker	Tulsa Webster	18	6-0	180	Leslie Van Noy

OKLAHOMA ALL-STATE FOOTBALL TEAM: 1949

SOUTH

Ends

Name	School	Age	Ht.	Wt.	Coach
Bob Brown	Sulphur	20	6-1	194	Jack Cox
Joe Gorley	Seminole	20	5-11	159	Gene Corrette
David Hester	Lawton	18	6-3	203	Glenn Dosser
Jack Spratt	Ardmore	17	6-2	186	George Holloway

Tackles

Name	School	Age	Ht.	Wt.	Coach
Jack Arnold	Elk City	18	6-0	206	Oscar Williams
Darrill Christian	Hollis	19	6-1	204	Joe B. Metcalf
Roger Nelson	Wynnewood	17	6-1	218	Tex Bartlett
Birch Rose	Norman	16	6-2	214	Doc LaFever

Guards

Name	School	Age	Ht.	Wt.	Coach
Tom Bear	Holdenville	17	5-10	222	John Daugherty
Raymond Jantz	Clinton	19	5-11	186	Otis Delaporte
Bob Murray	Wetumka	17	5-10	192	Hook Chowins
Bobby Tomah	Walters	16	5-11	171	J.D. Norton

Centers

Name	School	Age	Ht.	Wt.	Coach
Clint Chambers	Chickasha	18	6-0	194	L. D. Bash
Pat Fitter	Altus	17	6-2	184	Hal Hilpirt

Backs

Name	School	Age	Ht.	Wt.	Coach
Charles Kelly	Shawnee	18	5-10	161	Paul Greene
John Koch	OC Capitol Hill	18	6-0	176	John Miskovsky
Bob Miller	Seminole	18	5-11	156	Gene Corrette
Charles Murdock	OC Central	18	5-11	180	Jake Jacobson
Duane Reed	Clinton	18	5-9	163	Otis Delaporte
Dick Strong	McAlester	17	5-11	192	Dub Wooten
Jonnie Surrell	Atoka	17	5-10	162	Jack Murray
Jack Van Pool	OC Capitol Hill	17	6-0	171	John Miskovsky

OKLAHOMA ALL-STATE FOOTBALL TEAM: 1950

NORTH

Ends

Name	School	Age	Ht.	Wt.	Coach
Cloy Easley	Pawhuska	19	6-0	183	Lyle Yarbrough
Bob Grey	Tonkawa	18	6-1	184	Tom Turvey
Kenneth McCullough	Bartlesville	17	6-2	186	Burl Stidham
Vernon Womack	Fairview	16	6-1	197	George Eubanks

Tackles

Name	School	Age	Ht.	Wt.	Coach
Ned Blass	Ponca City	18	6-1	194	Earl Sullins
Kurt Burris	Muskogee	18	6-1	198	Paul Young
Joe Hilt	Cleveland	17	6-2	189	Joe Kerbel
Jim Holdridge	Stillwater	17	6-2	197	Ralph Tate
Don Howard	Newkirk	19	5-10	198	Carl Jackson

Guards

Name	School	Age	Ht.	Wt.	Coach
Don McGrew	Okmulgee	19	5-10	212	Bob Thomas
John Murrell	Fairfax	17	5-10	181	Ross Case
Jimmy Orr	Tulsa Rogers	17	5-8	199	Harry Knapp
James Yost	Vinita	18	6-2	194	Joe McGraw

Centers

Name	School	Age	Ht.	Wt.	Coach
Fallis Beall	Tulsa Webster	17	6-2	188	Carlos Clayton
Donald Payne	Collinsville	18	6-1	224	Frank Welch
Nelson Taylor	Thomas	17	5-11	178	Joe Ross

Backs

Name	School	Age	Ht.	Wt.	Coach
Max Boydston	Muskogee	18	6-2	183	Paul Young
Donald Bussey	Claremore	17	6-1	193	Paul Lovell
Bill Chitwood	Edmond	17	5-11	184	Al Blevins
Buddy Foreman	Bristow	18	6-1	177	Mose LeForce
Willard Fox	Broken Arrow	16	6-0	174	Herman Ragsdale
Lowell Harmon	Enid	17	5-9	179	Ed Brady
Bill Hawkins	Tulsa Central	17	6-0	171	Melvin Riggs
Elmer Manatowa	Cushing	17	5-7	156	Melvin Skelton
Johnny Sill	Stroud	18	6-2	193	Blue Gaither

OKLAHOMA ALL-STATE FOOTBALL TEAM: 1950

SOUTH

Ends

Name	School	Age	Ht.	Wt.	Coach
Dale Bryant	Mangum	19	6-2	192	Nate Watson
Ronnie Cordell	OC Central	18	6-2	181	Tub Jacobson
Bob LaRue	Clinton	17	6-2	182	Otis Delaporte
Hallard Randell	Antiers	18	6-0	178	Tom McVay

Tackles

Jackie Brooks	OC Capitol Hill	17	6-0	218	Jake Miskovsky
Earl Lynn	Putnam City	18	6-2	252	Jimmy Reynolds
James McGlothlin	Midwest City	18	6-2	214	Jake Spann
Ronald Thompson	Ada	17	6-0	206	Elvan George

Guards

Bill Hubbard	Hobart	17	6-1	186	Tip Jacobson
John Payne	Wewoka	17	5-10	209	Ciell Barnett
Bob Peters	Poteau	18	5-10	174	Sherman Floyd
Pat Thompson	Norman	17	5-10	167	Harley LaFevers
Bernard Wilson	Shawnee	18	5-11	197	Paul Greene

Centers

Donald Funk	Chickasha	17	6-0	184	Bobby Goad
Gene Mears	Seminole	18	6-3	178	Gene Corrotto
Wayne Wylie	Durant	17	6-1	182	Pete Tillman

Backs

Carl Allison	McAlester	17	6-0	192	Dub Wooten
Gene Dan Calame	Sulphur	17	5-10	171	Jack Cox
Jackie Dees	Lawton	17	5-7	153	Glenn Dosser
Buddy Donlev	OC Classen	17	5-11	189	Jim Conger
Carl Lawyer	OC Northeast	18	6-1	177	Cliff Speegle
Dale Lawyer	Holdenville	17	6-3	198	George Strickland
Wray Littlejohn	El Reno	17	6-1	195	Bob Bodenhamer
Artie Pucket	Sayre	18	6-0	179	Pop Kelly
Roy Randall	OC Capitol Hill	17	5-10	174	John Miskovsky

OKLAHOMA ALL-STATE FOOTBALL TEAM: 1951

NORTH

Ends

Name	School	Age	Ht.	Wt.	Coach
Lester Crawford	Blackwell	17	6-0	170	Chuck West
John LaFalier	Picher	17	5-11	180	John Adams
Bill Moody	Fairfax	19	5-11	165	Ross Case
Raymond Radcliff	Enid	17	6-0	170	Joe Gibson

Tackles

Name	School	Age	Ht.	Wt.	Coach
Virgil Bolinger	Muskogee	17	5-10	205	Paul Young
Don Kenney	Cushing	17	6-5	211	Melvin Skelton
Clyde Marsau	Tulsa Central	17	6-2	205	Melvin Riggs
Tom Ross	Ponca City	17	6-1	185	Earl Sullins
John Sain	Kingfisher	18	6-1	215	Burl Bartlett

Guards

Name	School	Age	Ht.	Wt.	Coach
Dick Claybaugh	Tulsa Rogers	17	6-1	205	Harry Knapp
Floyd Collins	Okmulgee	19	5-11	180	Bob Thomas
Don Resler	Cherokee	18	5-11	185	Floyd Gass
Ralph Studebaker	Perry	17	6-1	180	Bud Nichols

Centers

Name	School	Age	Ht.	Wt.	Coach
Walter Brecht	Sapulpa	18	6-0	190	Bom Bumgardner
Thurmond House	Tahlequah	18	6-0	175	Floyd Stierwait
Carl Rutledge	Woodward	17	5-11	160	L. D. Bash

Backs

Name	School	Age	Ht.	Wt.	Coach
Bob Andrew	Stillwater	17	6-0	170	Ralph Tate
Preston Carpenter	Muskogee	17	6-1	188	Paul Young
Pat Custar	Okemah	18	6-2	180	W. H. Wilson
Duane Goff	Newkirk	17	6-4	175	Carl Jackson
Jim Krider	Ponca City	17	6-0	185	Earl Sullins
Donny McDonald	Thomas	17	5-11	170	Joe Ross
L. C. Palmer	Sand Springs	17	5-10	150	Maurice Hail
David Rosengrant	Edmond	18	5-10	178	Al Blevins
Jimmy Wood	Pawnee	18	5-10	175	Gene Boyett

OKLAHOMA ALL-STATE FOOTBALL TEAM: 1951

SOUTH

Ends

Name	School	Age	Ht.	Wt.	Coach
Lloyd Carlisle	Sayre	18	6-0	170	Afton Kelley
Dick Earnest	Shawnee	16	6-3	190	Paul Greene
Ronald Horne	Ardmore	17	6-1	170	C. E. Jacobson
Jerry Scott	Ada	17	6-2	180	Elvan George

Tackles

Name	School	Age	Ht.	Wt.	Coach
Raymond Casey	Seminole	18	6-0	185	Gene Corrotto
Ronine Gandy	Temple	19	6-1	215	James Taylor
Hartsell Haws	Altus	17	5-11	190	Hal Hilpert
Wayne Litchfield	Wynnewood	18	6-1	190	Tex Bartlett

Guards

Name	School	Age	Ht.	Wt.	Coach
Monte Hendricks	Duncan	18	6-0	210	Earl Presley
Bob Hillis	Lawton	17	6-0	190	Glenn Dosser
Billy Jo Mitchell	Hollis	16	6-1	178	J. B. Metcalf
Bill Rogers	Clinton	19	5-10	175	Otis Delaporte
Pryor Waid	Waurika	17	5-10	195	Burl Thompson

Centers

Name	School	Age	Ht.	Wt.	Coach
Floyd Brown	OC Capitol Hill	18	5-11	190	C. B. Speegle
Don Gallop	Weatherford	18	6-3	192	Steve Graham
Bob Vance	El Reno	18	6-0	180	Bob Bodenhamer

Backs

Name	School	Age	Ht.	Wt.	Coach
Larry Adair	OC Central	19	6-3	210	Plato Andros
Mack Choate	Mangum	17	6-1	175	Nate Watson
John Compton	Anadarko	17	6-1	185	Frank Lucus
Leroy Courtney	OC John Marshall	17	6-2	195	Dick Noble
Tommy Greer	Duncan	17	5-11	155	Earl Presley
Tommy Murphy	OC Classen	18	5-10	170	Jim Conger
Paul Murray	Waurika	20	5-11	156	Burl Thompson
Bill Pierce	Chickasha	17	6-2	190	Harley Lafevers
Harvey Romans	Elk City	18	5-11	185	Vern Harris

OKLAHOMA ALL-STATE FOOTBALL TEAM: 1952

NORTH

Ends

Name	School	Age	Ht.	Wt.	Coach
John Bell	Enid	18	6-0	185	Joe Gibson
Jerry Dixon	Muskogee	18	6-0	175	Paul Young
T. J. Kennedy	Sapulpa	17	6-1	205	Bom Bomgardner
Bob Timberlake	Tulsa Central	17	6-0	180	Gene Corrette

Tackles

Fred Clarke	Ponca City	17	6-4	185	Earl Sullins
Bill Glynn	Nowata	17	6-1	225	John Brown
Mel Richeson	Cushing	20	5-10	175	Melvin Skelton
Chuck Yonkers	Henryetta	18	6-0	185	Lyle Berryhill

Guards

J. D. Irwin	Tonkawa	19	5-7	172	Travis Rhodes
Bob Krigbaum	Bartlesville	18	5-10	190	Burl Stidham
Barney Ramsey	Broken Arrow	18	5-10	190	Herman Ragsdale
Alfred Wolfe	Blackwell	18	6-2	195	Dub Wooten

Centers

Sonny Keys	Stillwater	18	6-3	190	Ralph Tate
Bob Phillips	Enid	17	5-11	174	Joe Gibson
J. B. Thompson	Hominy	17	6-2	205	Charles Shaw

Backs

Billy Brown	Wagoner	17	6-1	192	Cab Callaway
Robert Derrick	Woodward	18	6-0	175	L. D. Bash
Allen Fry	Claremore	17	5-8	157	Paul Lovell
Phil Harris	Elk City	17	5-11	176	Verne Harris
Delbert Long	Ponca City	17	5-10	165	Earl Sullins
Tom Moore	Cherokee	19	6-1	180	Floyd Gass
Billy Pricer	Perry	18	5-11	180	Bud Nichols
Donnie Vessels	Cleveland	19	5-10	174	W. Carmichael
John Wright	Sand Springs	17	5-10	165	Cecil Hankins
Bob Wyatt	Tulsa Central	17	5-11	175	Gene Corette

OKLAHOMA ALL-STATE FOOTBALL TEAM: 1952

SOUTH

Ends

Name	School	Age	Ht.	Wt.	Coach
Jim Ingram	OC Classen	19	5-11	185	Jim Conger
Tom Pearson	OC Capitol Hill	16	6-3	190	C. B. Speegle
Ted Watson	Shawnee	18	5-11	174	Paul Greene
Mike Willoughby	Ada	18	6-2	180	Elvan George

Tackles

Byron Beams	Ada	19	6-3	214	Elvan George
Gerald Benn	Sulphur	18	6-1	203	Jack Cox
John Smart	Midwest City	18	6-3	195	Jake Spann
Cloyd Sullins	OC Southeast	17	6-4	194	Bob Condren
Wyman Webster	Chickasha	17	6-1	205	Bud O'Des

Guards

Billy Davis	OC Capitol Hill	17	5-11	200	C. B, Speegle
Doc Herron	Mangum	17	5-9	190	Nate Watson
Billy Scott	Marlow	19	5-9	160	Sevil Pickett
R. L. "Duke" Wheeler	Tipton	17	5-10	164	Bennie Kennedy

Centers

Jim Mayfield	McAlester	17	6-2	180	Leon Manley
Bob Waugh	Norman	17	6-3	186	Pete Tillman

Backs

R. L. Cline	Weatherford	17	5-10	165	Steve Graham
George Day	Ardmore	18	6-1	190	Tip Jacobson
Dale DePue	OC Northeast	17	6-1	183	Carl Brewington
Jackie Evans	Clinton	18	5-10	170	Otis Delaporte
Hugh Morris	Midwest City	18	5-11	161	Jake Spann
Jay O'Neal	Ada	18	5-11	174	Elvan George
Bill Qualls	Poteau	19	6-3	194	Sherman Floyd
Don Wheatley	Lawton	18	5-8	158	Glenn Dosser
Dick Wilkins	Duncan	18	6-0	176	Earl Presley
Charles Wynes	El Reno	18	5-10	160	Bob Bodenhamer

OKLAHOMA ALL-STATE FOOTBALL TEAM: 1953

NORTH

Ends

Name	School	Age	Ht.	Wt.	Coach
Don Garner	Stillwater	17	6-1	175	Ralph Tate
Don Lee	Broken Arrow	19	6-1	175	Herman Ragsdale
Bob Witucki	Tulsa C. Hall	17	6-1	190	Lee Mahoney
Jack Wright	Tulsa Rogers	17	6-2	180	Bobby Goad

Tackles

James Barrett	Muskogee	18	5-11	185	Paul Young
Lou Boudreau	Shattuck	18	6-2	255	Mark Hodgson
Chuck Bowman	Ponca City	17	6-1	190	Earl Sullins
Larry Catherwood	Claremore	17	6-0	210	Paul Lovell
David Oates	Stillwater	17	6-0	210	Ralph Tate

Guards

J. R. Johnson	Tulsa Central	18	6-1	205	Don Slagle
Bob J. McAlester	Watonga	19	6-0	195	Dean Wild
Donnie Morris	Tulsa Webster	17	6-1	195	Bill McMichael
Jim Ware	Pawnee	17	5-10	190	Gene Boyett

Centers

Richard Cramer	Bartlesville	17	5-11	172	Burl Stidham
Gene Mullin	Ponca City	17	6-0	175	Earl Sullins

Backs

Jimmy Bourn	Tonkawa	17	6-0	178	Travis Rhodes
George Cook	Cushing	18	5-10	170	Melvin Skelton
Dale Duggins, Jr.	Stroud	19	6-2	192	Blue Gaither
Bill Edwards	Tulsa Rogers	17	6-1	190	Bobby Goad
James Heard	Cleveland	17	6-0	185	W. Carmichael
Leon Katapodis	Tulsa Central	18	5-10	165	Don Slagle
Ray Mantle	Commerce	17	6-1	178	Marshall Ishmael
Bill McDaniel	Enid	17	5-10	165	Charles Paine
Bill Sturm	Muskogee	17	5-9	158	Paul Young
Eugene Wheeler	Kingfisher	20	5-9	165	Burl Bartlett

OKLAHOMA ALL-STATE FOOTBALL TEAM: 1953

SOUTH

Ends

Name	School	Age	Ht.	Wt.	Coach
Tommy Fine	Lindsay	17	6-1	190	Tom Turvey
Dean McMasters	Chickasha	17	6-0	185	Bud O'Dea
Eddie Morton	Sulphur	18	5-11	170	Tracy Norwood
Don Stiller	Shawnee	17	6-3	200	Paul Greene

Tackles

Name	School	Age	Ht.	Wt.	Coach
Paul Haws	Altus	18	6-0	204	Art Young
Earl Johnson	El Reno	18	6-4	260	Bob Bodenhamer
Benton Ladd	OC Capitol Hill	18	6-1	220	C. B. Speegle
Bob Vanlandingham	Duncan	18	6-3	205	Earl Presley

Guards

Name	School	Age	Ht.	Wt.	Coach
Roland Butler	Poteau	17	6-1	195	Sherman Floyd
Kenneth Hallum	Seminole	18	6-0	200	Homer Simmons
Doyle Jennings	Lawton	17	6-0	205	Glenn Dosser
Bill Krisher	Midwest City	17	6-0	210	Jake Spann

Centers

Name	School	Age	Ht.	Wt.	Coach
Robert Greenhaw	Duncan	18	6-2	205	Earl Presley
Jim Jones	OC Central	17	6-2	194	Plato Andros
Roy King	Elk City	17	6-0	190	Ed Brady

Backs

Name	School	Age	Ht.	Wt.	Coach
George Church	Maysville	18	6-1	195	Tom McVay
Carl Dodd	Norman	18	6-0	185	J. L. Martin
Floyd Greenfield	Shawnee	18	6-2	192	Paul Greene
Charles Joseph	Seminole	18	6-1	179	Homer Simmons
Billy Joe Keesee	Hollis	19	5-10	170	Don Royal
Royce McQueen	Ardmore	18	6-3	180	Tip Jacobson
Chuck Page	OC Capitol Hill	17	5-10	165	C. B. Speegle
Don Smith	Sulphur	18	5-10	165	Tracy Norwood
Clendon Thomas	OC Southeast	17	6-2	195	Bob Condren
Ray Winn	Marlow	18	5-11	210	Sevil Pickett

OKLAHOMA ALL-STATE FOOTBALL TEAM: 1954

NORTH

Ends

Name	School	Age	Ht.	Wt.	Coach
Dick Brown	Wagoner	17	6-2	190	Alvin Duke
Joe Recter	Muskogee	17	6-0	180	Paul Young
John Rowden	Cushing	18	6-0	190	Melvin Skelton
Sam Shepherd	Tulsa Rogers	17	5-11	145	Bobby Goad

Tackles

Dan Erwin	Chandler	17	6-5	214	Shelby Wyatt
Kenneth Fitch	Bartlesville	17	6-0	210	Burl Stidham
Bob Sams	Jenks	17	6-2	225	Frank Herald
Bill Thompson	Henryetta	16	6-1	205	Lyle Berryhill
Irvin Wheeler	Alva	18	5-11	190	Bud Nichols

Guards

Lee Brady	Nowata	18	5-10	175	John Brown
Dick Gwinn	Tulsa Central	17	5-11	195	Don Slagle
Wesley Jordan	Ponca City	17	6-0	185	Earl Sullins
Ted Pendergraft	Cleveland	17	5-11	175	Bob Ford

Centers

Tom Harris	Cushing	17	5-10	194	Melvin Skelton
Roger Wickersham	Sand Springs	17	5-11	182	Cecil Hankins

Backs

Johnny Allen	Pawnee	19	5-11	175	Gene Boyett
Roy Boring	Ponca City	17	5-9	160	Earl Sullins
Ted Eakes	Broken Arrow	17	5-10	167	Joe Robinson
Bobby Green	Bartlesville	18	6-1	170	Burl Stidham
Melvin Howard	Laverne	17	5-10	180	Earl Kilmer
Don Jenkins	Tulsa Webster	17	6-1	204	Bill McMichael
Wayne Lenhart	OC John Marshall	18	5-8	150	Al Blevins
Jorge Madamba	Woodward	18	6-2	197	Wayne McGee
Don Ritschel	Tulsa Rogers	18	5-11	168	Bobby Goad
Olen Treadway	Muskogee	17	5-10	160	Paul Young

OKLAHOMA ALL-STATE FOOTBALL TEAM: 1954

SOUTH

Ends

Name	School	Age	Ht.	Wt.	Coach
Ross Coyle	Marlow	17	6-3	185	Sevil Pickett
Steve Jennings	Ardmore	18	6-2	190	Tip Jacobson
Bill Neal	Duncan	17	6-0	183	Harvey Griffin
DeWayne Owen	Seminole	16	6-0	165	Homer Simmons

Tackles

Name	School	Age	Ht.	Wt.	Coach
John Bowden	Poteau	19	6-3	218	Sherman Floyd
Dick Corbitt	Altus	17	6-2	205	Art Young
Jim Lawrence	Sayre	17	6-4	215	Afton Kelly
Ras McAdams	Ada	18	6-0	229	Elvan George
Danny Slagle	Okemah	18	6-1	207	W. H. Wilson

Guards

Name	School	Age	Ht.	Wt.	Coach
Dix Compton	Yukon	17	6-1	220	Jim Wade
Dan Ketchum	OC Classen	17	5-10	182	John Reddell
Tommy Wilson	Davis	18	6-0	182	Jack Riddie
Darrell Wooley	OC Capitol Hill	19	5-8	180	C. B. Speegle

Centers

Name	School	Age	Ht.	Wt.	Coach
Mickey Johnson	Comanche	17	6-2	202	Clee Beavers
Jim Nash	Wewoka	17	6-0	180	Phil Ball

Backs

Name	School	Age	Ht.	Wt.	Coach
Ray Boax	Altus	18	5-9	155	Art Young
Charlie Campbell	Talihina	18	5-8	163	Dick Moseley
Dick Evans	Midwest City	18	5-11	185	Jake Spann
Ronnie Jones	Lawton	17	5-10	159	Bob Bodenhamer
David Rolle	Poteau	18	6-1	195	Sherman Floyd
B. W. Scott	Ardmore	18	5-10	185	Tip Jacobson
Carl Slayton	OC Capitol Hill	17	6-1	185	C. B. Speegle
Dick Thrasher	Seminole	17	5-11	180	Homer Simmons
Dan Wagner	Ada	17	6-0	170	Elvan George
Duane Wood	Wilburton	17	6-1	185	Rudy Carney

OKLAHOMA ALL-STATE FOOTBALL TEAM: 1955

NORTH

Ends

Name	School	Age	Ht.	Wt.	Coach
Floyd Brown	Dewey	17	6-2	185	Tractor Trent
Don French	Sapulpa	17	6-2	185	B. Bomgardner
Berle Tate	Stilwell	17	6-2	185	Norvel Trask
Gene Yarbough	Guthrie	17	6-3	190	Lindell Pearson

Tackles

Buster Bradley	Cushing	17	5-11	235	Melvin Skelton
Richard Dupree	Tulsa Rogers	17	6-1	190	Bobby Goad
Don Eubanks	Fairfax	18	6-1	192	Ross Case
Lynn Pitts	Stillwater	17	6-1	210	Nate Watson

Guards

John Beaver	Morris	18	6-0	192	Bert Lana
Jodell Lewellen	Sand Springs	17	6-0	190	H. Wickersham
Don Straw	Nowata	18	6-0	225	John Brown
David Thayer	Blackwell	17	6-1	185	Burl Bartlett

Centers

Charles Cruce	Okemah	17	6-1	210	Noel Thomason
Jack Keller	Thomas	17	6-0	172	Joe Ross
Paul Southwick	Garber	18	6-0	200	Tex Bradshaw

Backs

Tony Banfield	Broken Arrow	16	6-2	168	Joe Robinson
Bob Brumble	Tulsa Rogers	18	5-11	175	Bobby Goad
Kelly Burden	Cushing	17	5-10	175	Melvin Skelton
Larry Carnes	Picher	17	6-0	212	Bo Spoon
Tommy Cotton	Pawhuska	17	5-11	180	Rosy Nolan
David Cross	OC Northeast	17	6-0	180	Johnny Walker
Jere Durham	Muskogee	17	6-0	190	Paul Young
Curtis LaPorte	Hennessey	18	5-11	165	Steve Stroud
Fred Trenary	Newkirk	17	6-2	195	Al Williamson
Dick Young	Sapulpa	18	5-9	155	B, Bomgardner

OKLAHOMA ALL-STATE FOOTBALL TEAM: 1955

SOUTH

Ends

Name	School	Age	Ht.	Wt.	Coach
John Burton	Seminole	17	6-0	160	H. Simmons
Bill Gary	Putnam City	17	6-2	180	Doc Graves
David George	Holdenville	17	6-2	190	John McKay
Bob McFarling	Shawnee	17	6-1	195	Jack Stogner

Tackles

Chuck Janssen	El Reno	17	6-0	195	Kenneth Kamm
Paul Potter	Elk City	19	6-0	200	Ed Brady
Jerry Thompson	Ada	17	5-9	193	Elvan George
Bob White	Poteau	17	6-1	210	Sherman Floyd

Guards

Scott Brown	Lawton	17	6-0	190	B. Bodenhamer
Jack Criswell	Wewoka	18	5-11	205	Phil Ball
Ronnie Hendricks	Duncan	18	5-11	193	Harvey Griffin
Billy Jack Moore	Ada	17	5-9	194	Elvan George
Delmas Thorne	Walters	17	5-11	188	Ralph Whiteley

Centers

Bill English	OC NW Classen	17	6-2	230	Rex Irwin
Fred Howard	McAlester	19	6-2	210	Doyle Long

Backs

Calvin Browning	Clinton	18	5-11	185	Carl Allison
Bill Garrett	Lindsay	17	5-11	165	Tom Turvey
Ronnie Hall	OC NW Classen	16	6-2	197	Rex Irwin
Brewster Hobby	Midwest City	18	5-9	175	Jim Darnell
Bobby Jobe	OC Capitol Hill	17	5-11	180	C. B. Speegle
John Paul Johnson	Ardmore	17	5-10	170	Tip Jacobson
Garye LaFevers	Chickasha	17	6-0	155	Bud O'Dea
Paul Payne	Wewoka	17	5-9	190	Phil Ball
Frankie Phelps	Wilburton	18	5-11	170	Jim Curtis
Glenn Sears	Healdton	18	6-2	200	Bill Wilson

OKLAHOMA ALL-STATE FOOTBALL TEAM: 1956

NORTH

Ends

Name	School	Age	Ht.	Wt.	Coach
Bill Cackler	Blackwell	18	6-1	185	Burl Bartlett
John Lung	Del City	17	6-4	195	Leo Presley
Bob Nix	Pryor	17	5-11	170	W. Carmichael
Ronald Vincent	Fairland	18	6-5	205	F. A. Dry
Stanley Ward	Stillwater	17	6-1	190	Nate Watson

Tackles

Name	School	Age	Ht.	Wt.	Coach
Paul Craig	Tulsa Rogers	17	6-3	190	Bobby Goad
Dallas Herzer	Sapulpa	18	6-0	210	B. Bomgardner
Pat Hutchens	Tulsa Rogers	17	6-2	190	Bobby Goad
Blanchard Reel	Okmulgee	17	6-1	182	Paul Lovell

Guards

Name	School	Age	Ht.	Wt.	Coach
Berry Harrison	Fairfax	17	6-2	206	Ross Case
Jim McGee	Stilwell	17	6-0	190	Norvel Trask
Paul Morrow	Perry	17	6-2	200	George Miller
Harvey Singer	Tulsa Central	17	5-11	190	Rosy Nolan

Centers

Name	School	Age	Ht.	Wt.	Coach
Jim Baker	Cushing	18	6-2	200	Melvin Skelton
Ron Henry	Henryetta	17	5-11	185	Lyle Berryhill

Backs

Name	School	Age	Ht.	Wt.	Coach
Willie Boyd	Cushing	20	6-0	190	Melvin Skelton
Jack Castin	Okmulgee	17	6-1	170	Paul Lovell
Joe Cheap	Buffalo	18	5-11	170	Tom Bice
Dick Dickerson	Guymon	17	6-0	180	Dick Noble
Paul Dudley	Sallisaw	17	6-0	168	K. McCormick
John Factor	Morris	18	5-8	160	Rex Sumner
Charles Gaither	Broken Arrow	19	5-10	170	Joe Robinson
Dick Jones	Stillwater	17	5-11	180	Nate Watson
Jerry Keeling	Enid	17	6-0	170	M. Vandaveer
Scotty Millington	Edmond	18	6-0	185	Bob Dever

OKLAHOMA ALL-STATE FOOTBALL TEAM: 1956

SOUTH

Ends

Name	School	Age	Ht.	Wt.	Coach
Barney Barnett	OC Northwest	17	6-2	185	Rex Irwin
James Dobson	OC Capitol Hill	17	6-2	195	C. B. Speegle
Frank Swafford	Norman	18	6-1	188	Buddy Brothers
Jerry Tillery	El Reno	18	6-2	195	Keneth Kamm

Tackles

Bill Brown	Frederick	18	6-2	195	Dean Wild
Walt Metcalfe	OC Northwest	17	6-4	210	Rex Irwin
Brent Morford	Lawton	17	6-3	235	B. Bodenhamer
Bill Watts	Putnam City	17	6-3	230	Joe Garrison

Guards

Bob Bannister	Altus	17	6-2	195	Art Young
Morris Menefee	OC Southeast	17	6-0	200	Bob Condren
Ronald Smith	Ardmore	18	6-1	194	Tip Jacobson
Charles Willingham	Lindsay	17	6-0	185	Tom Turvey

Centers

Bill Daniel	Midwest City	17	6-2	190	Jim Darnell
James Frazier	Ada	17	5-11	209	Elvan George
Lowell Watts	Duncan	17	5-11	188	Harvey Griffin

Backs

Larry Bahner	Ardmore	18	6-2	185	Tip Jacobson
Bill Brown	Holdenville	18	5-10	180	Gene Boyett
Jim Elliott	Elk City	17	5-8	150	Ed Brady
Ronnie Hartline	Lawton	18	6-2	193	B. Bodenhamer
Tommie Johnson	L. Douglass	18	5-10	171	H. C. King
Phil Lohmann	Pauls Valley	17	6-2	195	W. H. Wilson
Russell Perry	OC Douglass	17	6-0	175	M. F. Miller
Chester Pittman	Wewoka	19	5-9	165	Phil Ball
James Steward	Durant	18	5-10	190	Ralph Tate
Bob West	John Marshall	17	6-1	180	Al Blevins

OKLAHOMA ALL-STATE FOOTBALL TEAM: 1957

NORTH

Ends

Name	School	Age	Ht.	Wt.	Coach
Glen Cunningham	Bristow	17	6-4	185	Cal Woodworth
Fred Dobbins	Hominy	17	6-3	170	Al Simpler
Rusty Kraybill	Thomas	18	6-2	175	Joe Ross
R. C. Smith	Sapulpa	18	6-4	195	Chuck Boyle
David Wilks	Miami	17	6-1	185	Bo Bolinger

Tackles

Wilfred Bales	Tulsa Central	17	6-1	205	Rosy Nolan
Tim Crowley	Enid	17	6-3	210	M. Vandaveer
Ronald Rowden	Cushing	18	6-0	225	Melvin Skelton
Fred Staff	Pawnee	17	6-1	217	Max McKenzie

Guards

Benny Boydston	Muskogee	17	5-9	180	Paul Young
Bill McKinney	Bartlesville	17	6-0	195	Burl Stidham
James Stinnett	Chelsea	18	5-10	170	J. C. Ary
Jim Thompson	Okemah	18	6-0	190	Noel Thompson

Centers

Bob Blackburn	Claremore	17	6-3	195	Bear Jensen
Chris Bolton	Stillwater	18	6-2	190	Tom Turvey

Backs

George Aiken	Blackwell	17	5-11	165	Travis Rhodes
Billy Meacham	Clinton	18	5-11	170	Carl Allison
Don Anthony	Cushing	18	5-10	165	Melvin Skelton
Jerry Thompson	Stillwater	17	5-10	163	Tom Turvey
Eli Walker	Sapulpa	18	6-1	170	Chuck Boyle
Orville Bolinger	Muskogee	17	5-8	170	Paul Young
James Dillard	Fairfax	18	6-1	192	J. E. Landon
Mark Gibson	Bixby	18	6-2	190	Cliff Rogers
Ron MacDiarmid	Tulsa Rogers	17	5-9	175	Bobby Goad
Tex Yeager	Perry	18	6-0	187	George Miller

OKLAHOMA ALL-STATE FOOTBALL TEAM: 1957

SOUTH

Ends

Name	School	Age	Ht.	Wt.	Coach
Troy Freeman	Putnam City	17	6-0	180	Joe Garrison
Charles Hays	Ardmore	17	6-1	175	C. E. Jacobson
David Rice	Norman	17	6-2	180	Buddy Brothers
Wesley Stark	OC Capitol Hill	17	6-1	187	C. B. Speegle

Tackles

Leroy Corn	El Reno	17	6-0	190	Kenneth Kamm
Gary Cutsinger	Elk City	17	6-3	200	Ed Brady
Arnold Marshall	Lawton	18	6-1	210	Bob Bodenhamer
Maurice Severson	Midwest City	17	6-3	215	Jim Darnell
Henry Wells	Ada	17	6-3	220	Elvan George

Guards

Travis Hill	Henryetta	17	5-11	195	Lyle Berryhill
Jerry Moon	Lawton	17	5-10	185	Bob Bodenhamer
John Tiger	Seminole	17	5-9	165	Goob Arnold
Bobby Wyatt	Marlow	17	5-11	195	Sevil Pickett

Centers

Don Logan	Wewoka	17	5-10	170	Phil Ball
Woody McMahon	OC Grant	17	5-11	200	Tracy Norwood

Backs

David Harbour	Duncan	18	5-11	178	Harvey Griffin
DeWayne Pitt	Ada	17	5-11	190	Elvan George
Don Smith	Ardmore D.	17	6-1	158	T. M. Crisp
Ray Curtis	OC Capitol Hill	17	5-11	175	C. B. Speegle
Danny Griffin	Frederick	18	5-11	178	Dean Wild
Jack Hayden	OC Classen	17	5-8	155	Bob Mistole
Bob Irvin	Poteau	17	6-0	170	Sherman Floyd
Jim Murphy	El Reno	17	6-0	185	Kenneth Kamm
Richard Sinclair	Harding	17	5-10	155	Jerry Pelter
Ronnie Dombek	Henryetta	17	6-2	190	Lyle Berryhill

OKLAHOMA ALL-STATE FOOTBALL TEAM: 1958

NORTH

Ends

Name	School	Age	Ht.	Wt.	Coach
Kenneth Eddy	Checotah	17	6-2	200	Harold Latham
Dale Feltenberger	Nowata	17	6-1	180	John Brown
Bill Hodges	Blackwell	17	6-3	170	Travis Rhodes
Grover Marshall	Bartlesville	17	6-2	192	Burl Stidham

Tackles

David Adams	Tulsa Rogers	17	6-1	214	Chuck Boyle
Bud Coffman	Perry	17	6-2	218	Ben Niles
Larry Crowdis	Thomas	17	6-1	205	Joe Ross
Curt Dobbins	Hominy	17	6-0	220	Jim Crossland
Jim Taylor	Miami	18	6-3	200	Dorsey Gibson

Guards

Tommy Adams	Sapulpa	17	5-11	200	Ed Brady
Gary Cole	Guthrie	17	5-9	200	Bob Daugherty
Tony Kilgore	Muskogee	17	5-10	165	Paul Young
Bob Robertson	Crescent	17	5-10	210	George Dickey

Centers

Tom Webb	Tulsa Edison	17	6-3	227	Ralph Parker
Laron Dozier	Okmulgee D.	17	5-11	185	Elmer House

Quarterbacks

Val Reneau	Cushing	17	5-10	185	Melvin Skelton
Ken White	Tulsa Edison	16	5-9	160	Ralph Parker

Halfbacks

Bob Bruno	Tulsa Central	17	5-11	165	Rosy Nolan
Don Derrick	Woodward	18	6-0	175	Phil Smith
Eddie Huggins	Grove	17	5-9	170	Paul Davis
Steve Johnson	Pryor	17	6-0	175	W. Charmichael
Dwayne Parent	Fairfax	18	601	182	J. E. Landon

Fullbacks

Ronnie Harmon	Cushing	17	5-9	170	Melvin Skelton
John Porterfield	Bixby	17	6-1	190	Max McKenzie
Jim Stockard	Sapulpa	17	5-11	170	Ed Brady

OKLAHOMA ALL-STATE FOOTBALL TEAM: 1958

SOUTH

Ends

Name	School	Age	Ht.	Wt.	Coach
Charles Johnson	Ardmore D.	16	6-3	204	Frank Luster
Jerry McMillan	OC Grant	17	6-1	180	T. Norwood
Tom Swineford	Chickasha	17	5-11	170	George Elliott
Larry Waller	Lawton	17	6-0	185	B. Bodenhamer

Tackles

H. O. Estes	Lindsay	17	6-2	193	V. Robertson
Claude Hamon	Harding	17	6-5	205	Jerry Potter
Don Keeton	Shawnee	17	6-2	215	Dick Bowman
Rodney Replogle	McAlester	17	6-1	205	Hook Eales
John Sowers	Seminole	17	6-5	205	Phil Ball

Guards

Wayne Cargill	Norman	18	5-11	180	Gene Corrotto
Bert Elliott	OC Capitol Hill	18	5-11	173	C. B. Speegle
Jim Mihlhauser	Lindsay	17	5-10	210	V. Robertson
Gene Whatley	Duncan	17	6-0	190	Harvey Griffin

Centers

Bill Puckett	OC Northeast	17	6-0	175	H. Merideth
Gary Webb	Putnam City	18	6-3	225	Joe Garrison

Quarterbacks

Bruce Long	Ada	17	6-2	178	Elvan George
Don Trull	OC Southeast	17	6-1	170	Dean Choate

Halfbacks

Ed Nowlin	OC Capitol Hill	18	5-11	180	C. B. Speegle
Melvin Sandersfeld	Hobart	17	6-3	180	Tex Bartlett

Fullbacks

Dallas Barnett	Harding	17	6-1	188	Jerry Potter
Dean Bass	Moore	18	6-2	190	Bob Holder
Buzz McDonald	OC Northwest	17	5-8	172	Rex Irwin
Pete Payne	Wewoka	17	5-10	185	N. Thomason
Dick Speir	Grandfield	17	5-10	170	Don Shadid
Bill Willis	Ada	17	5-10	194	Elvan George

OKLAHOMA ALL-STATE FOOTBALL TEAM: 1959

NORTH

Ends

Name	School	Ht.	Wt.	Coach
Randolph Furch	Boggs	6-3	203	Jim Marshall
John Garrett	Stilwell	6-3	205	Frank Mobra
Larry Hill	Guymon	6-1	211	Dick Noble
George Tasar	Tulsa Edison	6-2	200	Ralph Parker

Tackles

Jack Brisco	Blackwell	6-1	205	Travis Rhodes
Kelly Hampton	Groves	6-3	205	Al Hamra
Ray Taylor	Tulsa Central	6-2	200	Rosey Nolan
Mike Upton	Stillwater	6-1	195	Tom Turvey

Guards

Charles Bush	Beaver	5-11	180	Tom McVay
Palmer Koontz	Tulsa Central	5-11	185	Rosey Nolan
Jim Nash	Okmulgee D.	5-11	191	Elmer House
Nick Oakley	Muskogee	6-0	190	Paul Young

Centers

Jack Blackburn	Checotah	6-1	205	Harold Latham
Mike Tanner	Claremore	6-2	190	Bear Jensen

Backs

Jerry Lawhorn	Bixby	5-10	176	Lee Snider
Bill Van Burklee	Tulsa Rogers	5-11	185	Chuck Boyle
Jerry Ellis	Blackwell	6-0	180	Travis Rhodes
Bill Harper	Woodward	6-2	185	Jim Crossland
Joe Phillips	Guymon	6-0	176	Dick Noble
Mac Plummer	Enid	6-0	165	Harvey Griffin
Ken Rader	Hominy	6-0	180	Woody Cooper
Larry Ballard	Claremore	5-11	175	Bear Jensen
Glen Condren	Muldrew	6-3	205	Perry Lattimore
Jim Stevenson	Muskogee	6-2	180	Paul Young
Mike Veclaw	Bartlesville	5-11	190	Burl Stidham

OKLAHOMA ALL-STATE FOOTBALL TEAM: 1959

SOUTH

Ends

Name	School	Ht.	Wt.	Coach
Gene Abney	Marlow	6-1	175	Sevil Pickett
Doyle Ivestser	Wewoka	6-0	198	Noel Thomason
Mack Kuykendall	Anadarko	6-3	192	Bob Delver
Tom Ward	OC Northwest	6-2	192	Rex Irwin

Tackles

Jerry Goldsby	Norman	6-1	182	Gene Corrette
Bob Howard	Lawton	6-0	195	Bob Bodenhamer
George Metcalfe	Harding	6-2	195	Jerry Potter
George Stokes	Madill	6-4	210	Bill Ayres
Larry Vermillion	Chickasha	5-10	205	George Elliott

Guards

Wayne Clark	Midwest City	5-11	205	Jim Darnell
Bobby Ford	Clinton	6-1	205	Otis Delaporte
Jim Jackson	McAlester	6-1	185	Hook Eales
Larry Taylor	OC Capitol Hill	6-1	222	C. B. Speegle, Jr.

Centers

Danny Eoff	Duncan	6-0	185	Earl Presley
Tom Farris	OC Grant	6-0	208	Tracy Norwood
Jack Jacobson	Ardmore	6-1	180	Tip Jacobson

Backs

Preston Holsinger	Lawton	5-10	160	Bob Bodenhamer
Mike Miller	OC Northwest	6-1	172	Rex Irwin
C. B. Speegle, III	OC Capitol Hill	5-9	163	C. B. Speegle, Jr.
Jay Wilkinson	Norman	6-0	190	Gene Corrette
Lewis Borders	Allen	6-1	193	Ray Schofield
Jackie Cowan	OC Northeast	5-10	172	Harold Merideth
Charles Mayhue	Ada	5-11	178	Craig McBroom
Wayne Scott	Marlow	5-11	160	Sevil Pickett
Eddie Shegog	Lawton Douglass	6-2	185	William Lee

OKLAHOMA ALL-STATE FOOTBALL TEAM: 1960

NORTH

Name	School	Pos.	Ht.	Wt.
Walter Depew	Beaver	E	6-0	195
Wempsey Gilkey	Pawhuska	E-HB	5-10	155
Paul Harjo	Henryetta	E	6-2	195
J. D. Robinson	Miami	E-FB	6-2	208
Dale Pontius	Blackwell	T-FB	6-2	194
Jim Speaks	Woodward	T	5-11	185
Don Stevens	OC Star Spencer	T	6-0	212
David Brown	Claremore	G	5-11	185
Marcus Hendricks	Claremore	G	5-10	175
Ron Lowry	Edmond	G	5-10	190
Frank Forbes	Ponca City	G-C	5-9	190
Mike Long	Tulsa Central	C	6-2	190
Jim Morrison	Tulsa Rogers	C	5-10	184
Lylin Cowan	Checotah	QB-HB	5-10	165
Jeff Jordan	Bristow	QB	6-3	170
Petee Mosely	Miami	HB	5-11	188
Randy Rudisell	Bartlesville	HB	6-0	180
Jon Running	Tulsa Edison	HB	5-9	170
David Voiles	Hooker	LB-FB	6-1	195
Darrell Wolfe	Cushing	LB-FB	5-8	160
Ronnie Derrick	Woodward	FB	6-3	195
Jack London	Tulsa Rogers	FB	6-0	175
Harry Red Eagle	Hominy	FB	6-2	195
West Skidgel	Cleveland	FB	5-10	175
Robert Temple	Choctaw	FB	5-11	172

OKLAHOMA ALL-STATE FOOTBALL TEAM: 1960

SOUTH

Name	School	Pos.	Ht.	Wt.
Allen Bumgardner	Putnam City	E	6-1	200
Dan Hood	Ada	E	6-0	205
Rick McCurdy	Purcell	E	6-3	195
Robert Taylor	OC Southeast	E	6-1	175
Don Byrd	Ada	T	5-10	195
Danny Clanton	Blanchard	T	6-0	185
Roddy Cutsinger	Elk City	T	6-2	208
Larry Ferguson	Lawton	T	6-0	205
Jim Maxwell	Stigler	T	6-1	205
Roger Newberry	Elk City	T	6-2	202
Ted Dodson	Midwest City	G	5-11	195
Lee Spencer	Shawnee	G	5-10	190
Bennie Cravatt	Harding	C	6-0	180
Jim Carriger	McAlester	C	6-1	195
Don Bateman	OC Southeast	QB	6-0	185
James Ferrell	Seminole	QB	6-0	160
Tom Pannell	Norman	QB	5-10	162
Jerry Johnston	Heavener	QB-HB	5-10	160
Preston Bagley	Midwest City	HB	6-0	178
Arthur Guess	OC Central	HB	5-8	155
Gary Livingston	Norman	HB	5-10	165
Greg Burns	Putnam City	FB	6-0	202
David McKinney	Seminole	FB	6-1	190
Donnie Parish	Idabel	FB	5-11	182
George Thomas	OC Douglass	FB	5-11	206

OKLAHOMA ALL-STATE FOOTBALL TEAM: 1961

NORTH

Name	School	Pos.	Ht.	Wt.
Bob Bigelow	Tulsa Edison	E-HB	6-0	183
Dwight Claxton	Coweta	E-QB	6-1	182
Bruce Bettis	Bartlesville	T	6-3	215
Vernon Burkett	Muskogee	T	5-11	182
Gip Duggan	Choctaw	T	5-11	205
Rusty Martin	Checotah	T	6-0	210
Tom Myattt	Newkirk	T	6-1	205
Alonzo Edwards	Tulsa Washington	G	5-10	195
Charles Harper	Broken Arrow	G-FB	6-0	200
Don Mellott	Tulsa Rogers	G-FB	6-1	198
Willie Swan	Enid	G	5-11	195
Don Kindley	Cushing	C	6-2	180
Woodie Berry	Stillwater	QB	5-9	165
Curt Cook	Tulsa Rogers	QB	6-2	182
Jim Graham	Tulsa Edison	QB	5-7	160
John Hammond	Tulsa Central	QB	6-1	170
Jay Hurt	Pawhuska	QB	5-10	170
Larry Brown	Jenks	HB	5-11	195
Richard Keller	Thomas	HB	5-11	172
Willie Ozbirn	Edmond	HB	6-1	190
Don Smith	Tulsa Central	HB	6-1	180
Mickey Upton	Stillwater	HB	5-10	168
Skip Baird	Beaver	FB	5-11	185
Phil Brooks	Tulsa Hale	FB	6-1	190
Joe Lane	Vinita	FB	6-1	195

OKLAHOMA ALL-STATE FOOTBALL TEAM: 1961

SOUTH

Name	School	Pos.	Ht.	Wt.
Thurman Edwards	Seminole	E	6-0	188
Bill Thomas	Lawton	E-QB	6-3	195
Jim Whipple	OC Capitol Hill	E	6-1	185
Joe Brooks	Pauls Valley	T	6-3	220
Bill Flanagan	Walters	T	5-11	194
John McCray	Norman	T	5-10	185
Bob Metcalfe	Harding	T	6-4	210
Carl Smith	Wynnewood	T	5-11	190
Bob Watts	Putnam City	T	6-1	230
Pet Francis	Midwest City	G	6-1	210
Irvin Roley	Norman	G	5-11	160
Jim Click	Altus	C	6-1	185
Bill Pennington	Duncan	C	6-2	178
Ronnie Engel	Elk City	QB	6-1	184
John Goodner	Frederick	QB	6-0	180
Thurman Pitchlynn	Wewoka	QB	5-11	180
Mike Ringer	Pauls Valley	QB	6-1	180
Mike Wood	Ada	QB	5-8	165
Richard Cole	Stigler	HB	6-1	175
Jim Doolittle	McAlester	HB	6-0	190
Larry Elliott	Elk City	HB	5-7	155
Royce Fisher	Ada	HB	5-6	150
Hilliard Shackford	Harding	HB	5-7	165
Tommy Bell	OC Southeast	FB	5-10	180
Hugh McCrabb	OC Northeast	FB	6-0	187

OKLAHOMA ALL-STATE FOOTBALL TEAM: 1962

NORTH

Name	School	Pos.	Ht.	Wt.
Bill Beierschmitt	Alva	E-QB	6-1	180
Rod Goodsell	Tulsa Rogers	E	6-1	180
Bill Ross	Tulsa Edison	E-FB	6-0	193
Mike Base	Geary	T	6-0	205
George Botts	Miami	T	6-1	205
Carl Chew	Dewey	T	5-11	222
Larry Donley	Woodward	T	6-4	225
Richard Haynes	Sapulpa	T	5-11	205
Dennis Randell	Tulsa McLain	T	6-5	210
James Riley	Enid	T	6-2	205
Omer Sumter	Claremore	T	6-1	230
Pat Gordon	Tulsa Central	C	5-11	190
Donnie McVay	Beaver	C-FB	6-0	185
Rick Goodman	Choctaw	QB	6-2	190
Gary Moore	Tulsa Hale	QB	5-10	165
Stu Berryhill	Cleveland	HB	5-11	175
Fred Cheek	Vinita	HB	5-10	160
Rodney Crosswhite	Hennessey	HB	5-10	170
Stan Crowder	Enid	HB	5-11	175
Richard Dunlap	Skiatook	HB	6-1	181
Jim Mudd	Berryhill	HB	5-8	175
Gene Stephenson	Guthrie	HB	5-11	175
Larrry Crutchner	Okmulgee	FB	6-0	205
Jon Kennedy	Ponca City	FB	6-0	225
David Stevenson	Muskogee	FB	6-0	170

OKLAHOMA ALL-STATE FOOTBALL TEAM: 1962

SOUTH

Name	School	Pos.	Ht.	Wt.
Dale Davis	Marlow	E	6-3	195
Curt Holdridge	Altus	E-C	6-2	187
Scottie Long	Lawton	E	6-2	193
Clyde McGill	Marietta	T	6-2	195
Dennis Adams	Harding	T	5-10	187
Robert Kalsu	Del City	T	6-5	215
Jim Nievar	OC Capitol Hill	T	6-1	225
Gary Barr	Clinton	G	5-10	182
Bud Townsend	Putnam City	C	5-10	185
Larry Allford	McAlester	G-G	5-11	205
Doug Kemper	Lawton	C-T	6-0	194
Charles Krause	Ada	C-LB	6-0	172
Doug Cathey	Ryan	QB	5-11	180
Bob Looney	Harding	QB	6-1	185
Ken Stockdale	Ardmore	QB	5-11	170
Gipp DuPree	OC Northwest	QB	5-10	160
Ben Hart	OC Douglass	HB	6-2	200
Gary King	Norman	HB	5-10	160
Jerry Gill	Lindsay	HB	5-11	170
Gary Phillips	Ada	HB	5-9	165
Mack Steele	Spiro	HB	5-8	150
Gill Wright	OC Northwest	HB	5-9	170
Larry Leeds	OC John Marshall	FB	5-9	165
Eugene Ross	Clinton	FB-E	6-2	187
Harvey Tisdale	Lawton McArthur	FB	5-11	187

OKLAHOMA ALL-STATE FOOTBALL TEAM: 1963

NORTH

Name	School	Pos.	Ht.	Wt.
Ron Bowles	Tulsa Webster	E	6-0	192
Don Frank	Stillwater	E	6-3	175
Jim Little	Muskogee	E-G	5-10	165
Wes Butts	Jenks	T	6-0	165
Tom Corr	Enid	T	5-10	200
Pete Davis	Okmulgee	T	6-2	219
Marshall Dicks	Claremore	T-G	6-1	188
Roland Hula	Medford	G	6-0	187
David Self	Thomas	G-HB	5-11	190
Granville Liggins	Tulsa Washington	T-G	5-11	210
John Matlock	Stillwater	T	6-1	195
Charles McMath	Broken Arrow	T	6-1	195
Rusty Goodsell	Tulsa Rogers	C	6-1	205
Charles Miller	Dewey	C	5-11	185
Jim Linn	Tulsa Hale	QB	5-11	170
Dan Shane	Henryetta	QB-E	6-2	185
Larry Atkinson	Beaver	HB	5-8	170
Milton Bassett	Woodward	HB	5-10	165
Bob Davisson	Drumright	HB	5-10	175
Richard Nash	Nowata	HB	5-10	175
Don Sandmire	Miami	HB	5-11	165
Roy Wallace	Claremore	HB	5-11	175
Tom Boone	Moreland	FB	6-1	180
Scott Hall	Tulsa Edison	FB	6-0	195
Joe Poslick	Enid	FB	6-0	210

OKLAHOMA ALL-STATE FOOTBALL TEAM: 1963

SOUTH

Name	School	Pos.	Ht.	Wt.
Leonard Arnold	OC Capitol Hill	E	6-1	180
Eddie Lancaster	Shawnee	E	6-1	205
Kenneth Wallace	Lawton McArthur	E	6-1	195
Bob Kelso	Ada	T	5-11	210
Dave King	Lindsay	T	6-0	210
Gary Mixon	Idabel	T	6-1	195
Danny Murdock	Harding	T	6-1	205
Jack Taliaferro	Duncan	T	6-4	215
Gary Simmons	OC John Marshall	T	6-1	190
Keith Lavender	Lawton	G	5-9	174
Ashley Rutherford	Midwest City	G	5-9	175
Dean Tom	Marlow	G	5-11	195
Bob Craig	McAlester	C	6-1	205
Dick Lerbalance	Hartshorne	C	6-1	215
Jim Burgar	Lindsay	QB	6-0	175
Buddy Burris	Putnam City	QB	5-11	170
Gene Cagle	Lawton	QB	5-11	174
Frank Hester	Clinton	HB	5-9	175
Jerry Lee	McAlester	HB	5-7	150
Bobby Murcer	OC Southeast	HB	5-10	155
Jerry Pitt	OC Grant	HB	6-1	175
Ron Shotts	Weatherford	HB	6-0	200
Scott Pelton	Marlow	FB	5-11	195
Stanley Thomas	Durant	FB	6-1	220
Willie Wystemp	OC John Marshall	FB	6-0	197

OKLAHOMA ALL–STATE FOOTBALL TEAM: 1964

NORTH

Name	School	Pos.	Ht.	Wt.
Phil Angeri	Tulsa Hale	E	5-11	184
Ken Russell	Perry	E-HB	6-1	190
Ned Williams	Vian	E-FB	6-1	212
Jim Basden	Henryetta	T	6-2	235
Brad Baughman	Bartlesville	T	6-0	210
Terry Donley	Woodward	T-C	6-3	230
Ronald Freeman	Muskogee	T	5-11	185
Jim Hunt	Pawhuska	T-FB	6-1	197
Tom Merritt	Pryor	T	6-0	185
Phil Tuttle	Guymon	G	5-11	195
Don Undernehr	Tulsa Webster	G	5-9	205
Jon Kolb	Owasso	G-E	6-3	208
Dale Patterson	Okmulgee	C	5-10	205
Mike Arnold	Enid	QB	5-11	170
Paul Hull	Tulsa Rogers	QB	5-8	148
Ron Johnson	Stillwater	QB	6-0	172
Danny Bradberry	Spiro	HB	5-10	180
Gary Harper	Jenks	HB	6-1	202
Ronald McCrary	Bristow	HB	6-2	180
Dean Price	Copan	HB	5-10	165
Harry Wood	Tulsa Memorial	HB	6-0	160
Richard Escoe	Enid	FB	5-11	180
David Ladner	Ponca City	FB	6-0	198
Vic Prather	Tulsa Rogers	FB	6-2	190
Danny Willis	Bixby	FB	5-11	185

OKLAHOMA ALL-STATE FOOTBALL TEAM: 1964

SOUTH

Name	School	Pos.	Ht.	Wt.
John Campbell	Norman	E	5-11	170
Randy Meacham	Clinton	E	6-3	218
Dean Pierce	OC Northeast	E	6-2	205
Larry Roberts	Marietta	E-QB	6-1	191
Gene Davis	Midwest City	T	6-3	220
Charles Newton	Altus	T	6-3	225
Terry Whatley	Duncan	T	6-2	220
Jim Fletcher	Ada	T-G	6-0	218
Danny Noles	Lindsay	T-G	5-11	205
Brad Avant	Bethany	G	5-8	180
Jim Norwood	Idabel	G-FB	6-0	195
Phil Pratt	Pauls Valley	C-T	6-0	205
Chuck Williams	Ardmore	C	6-0	190
Ricky Bridges	Lawton Eisenhower	QB	5-9	160
Chebon Dacon	OC Capitol Hill	QB	6-0	170
Freeman Harris	Broken Bow	QB	5-11	165
Bob Harvey	OC John Marshall	QB	6-0	175
Joe Logan	Norman	QB	6-0	185
Bob Warmack	Ada	QB	6-0	165
Johnny Webber	Hartshorne	QB	6-2	190
SanToi DeBose	OC Star Spencer	HB	6-1	185
Larry Gosney	Crooked Oak	HB	6-0	205
Eddie Hinton	Lawton	HB	6-1	182
Terry Brown	Marlow	FB	6-0	175
Rick McCoin	Holdenville	FB	6-2	200

OKLAHOMA ALL-STATE FOOTBALL TEAM: 1965

NORTH

Name	School	Pos.	Ht.	Wt.
Joe Esch	Tonkawa	E-FB	6-0	185
Bill Fisher	Tahlequah	E	6-3	203
Mike Hendren	Muskogee	E	6-4	198
Ernie Renfrow	Stigler	E	6-3	170
Ralph Wilson	Waynoka	E	6-1	193
Howard Cobb	Newkirk	T	6-1	205
Dale Nichols	Broken Bow	T	6-0	210
Bob Plummer	Hominy	T	5-11	215
John Ward	Tulsa Rogers	T	6-4	219
James Kelly	Choctaw	G	6-0	195
Mike Nolan	Tulsa Memorial	G	5-10	205
John Giles	Bixby	C	6-2	185
Ken Mendenhall	Enid	C	6-1	190
Robert Cutburth	Tulsa Webster	QB	6-0	200
Pat Herald	Jenks	QB-HB	5-11	190
Doug Matthews	Picher	QB	5-9	162
Mickey Ripley	Perry	QB	6-1	175
Terry Chaloupek	Seiling	HB	5-8	178
Donnie Fowler	Woodward	HB	5-8	160
Joey Grayson	Tulsa Rogers	HB	5-10	180
Steve Owens	Miami	HB	6-2	197
Kent Grant	Stillwater	FB	6-0	190
Emery Hicks	Nowata	FB	5-11	201
Spencer Kissell	Bartlesville	FB	6-1	200
Odell Lawson	Ponca City	FB	6-3	185

OKLAHOMA ALL-STATE FOOTBALL TEAM: 1965

SOUTH

Name	School	Pos.	Ht.	Wt.
Miles Hall	Midwest City	E	6-4	210
Bob Hill	Marlow	E	6-3	210
Joe Killingsworth	OC Southeast	E	6-3	183
David Klumb	OC Star Spencer	E	5-11	190
Jerry Bostic	Wynnewood	T	6-1	228
Larry Daniel	Hugo	T	6-1	225
Jerry Dossey	Lawton	T	6-4	215
Gary Mead	Lawton Eisenhower	T	6-2	185
Steve Merida	Altus	T	6-1	205
Bruce Click	Ada	G	6-0	180
Gary Darnell	Moore	G	6-0	185
Jim Peters	Wynnewood	G	6-0	220
Ted Shadid	Shawnee	G	6-3	225
Wesley Brown	McAlester	C	6-2	222
John Johnson	OC Northwest	C	6-0	195
Jim Caster	Altus	QB	5-10	165
Bob Murphy	Midwest City	QB	6-3	198
Ronnie Jones	OC Capitol Hill	QB-HB	5-11	175
Paul Blevins	Norman	HB	5-9	168
Jerry Garner	Poteau	HB	6-3	190
Jerry Heatherington	Panama	HB	5-11	185
Pat Kernan	OC John Marshall	HB	5-8	160
Rick Baldridge	Lawton	FB	6-1	205
Carlos Bell	Clinton	FB	6-5	225
Ken Fleming	Lindsay	FB	6-2	199

OKLAHOMA ALL-STATE FOOTBALL TEAM: 1966

NORTH

Name	School	Pos.	Ht.	Wt.
Tom Dearinger	Stillwater	E	6-2	185
Roger Dicus	Bixby	E	6-4	205
Scott Van Krevelin	Enid	E	6-0	185
John Watson	Tulsa McLain	E	6-5	205
Clarence Newton	Tulsa Washington	E-T	6-3	205
Joe Breshears	Vinita	T	6-3	205
Alger Flood	Okmulgee	T-C	6-4	215
Mike Goldberg	Tulsa Edison	T	6-3	220
Eddie Lawrence	Nowata	T	5-10	208
Bill Luttrell	Perry	T	6-0	220
Ron Stacy	Pryor	T	6-4	205
Tom Arnold	Tulsa Rogers	G	6-0	190
Mike Dupree	Tulsa Rogers	G	5-11	215
John Harleson	Okemah	C	6-2	195
Gene Niles	Perkins	C	6-2	195
Dale Holt	Enid	QB	6-0	170
Woody Roof	Thomas	QB	5-11	190
Charles Wilson	Broken Arrow	QB	6-4	175
Forb Phillips	Tulsa Hale	QB-HB	6-1	188
Gene Barnes	Garber	HB	6-1	170
Eddie Humphrey	Sapulpa	HB	5-9	190
David Slatton	Sand Springs	HB	6-1	188
Bo Smith	Vinita	HB	6-0	175
Dru Allcorn	Tulsa McLain	FB	6-1	215
Bob Nichols	Tulsa Edison	FB	6-2	198

OKLAHOMA ALL-STATE FOOTBALL TEAM: 1966

SOUTH

Name	School	Pos.	Ht.	Wt.
Joe Coyle	Rush Springs	E	6-1	200
Danny Hardaway	Lawton	E	6-3	201
Clifford Jefferson	Clinton	E	5-11	185
Greg Pinkerton	Putnam City	E	5-11	170
David Gaile	OC Grant	T	6-0	198
Mike Gamble	Spiro	T	6-0	210
Randy Lawrence	Duncan	T	6-3	205
June Spivey	OC Central	T	6-1	215
Ed Stewart	Wilson	T	6-4	245
Lloyd Whitfield	Pauls Valley	T	6-3	200
Duck Johnson	Ardmore	G	6-0	190
Eddie Miller	Wewoka	G	5-10	185
Tommy Noles	Lindsay	G	5-11	195
Tom Peters	Altus	C	6-3	197
Ron Robinson	Crooked Oak	C	5-11	190
Ernest Sheppard	Lawton Eisenhower	QB	6-2	180
Wayne Ward	Talihina	QB	5-11	160
Glen Castle	OC Southeast	QB-HB	5-9	170
Steve Choate	OC Northwest	HB	5-9	150
Ronnie Cothren	Wynnewood	HB	6-2	173
Dale Holland	El Reno	HB	5-9	180
Jim Quick	Ardmore	HB	5-10	185
Rick Thompson	Shawnee	HB	5-10	177
Milton King	Yukon	FB	6-0	185
Steve West	Ada	FB	6-1	205

OKLAHOMA ALL-STATE FOOTBALL TEAM: 1967

NORTH

Name	School	Pos.	Ht.	Wt.
Jim Butler	Skiatook	E	6-3	195
Harry Case	Tulsa Rogers	E	6-1	195
John McGivern	Tulsa Kelley	E	6-2	170
Pat Wilsey	Stillwater	E	6-0	180
Steve butler	Wagoner	T-FB	6-2	205
Frank Creamer	Tulsa Hale	T	6-1	205
Mark Driscoll	Ponca City	T-LB	6-0	190
Louis McGee	Stilwell	T	6-3	230
Bill Kilpatrick	Muskogee	T	6-1	210
Art Ruby	Tulsa Central	T-C	6-2	205
Randy Matlock	Stillwater	G	5-10	180
Pat Bell	Okmulgee	G-C	6-1	180
Bob Clinard	Harrah	C	5-11	180
Rodney Randall	Broken Arrow	C	5-11	200
Bruce Jones	Stroud	QB	6-3	180
Scott Martin	Bartlesville College	QB	5-11	175
James Stuemky	Newkirk	QB	6-2	175
Floyd Tiger	Tulsa Washington	QB	5-10	185
Terry Ballard	Okmulgee	HB	5-8	170
Gilbert Barnes	Balko	HB	6-1	195
Kent Bays	Tulsa Memorial	HB	6-0	165
Gilbert Horton	Vian	HB	6-2	185
Oliver Zeigler	Tulsa Washington	HB	5-9	165
Fred Sander	Seiling	FB	5-11	195
Les Williams	Enid	FB	6-0	190

OKLAHOMA ALL-STATE FOOTBALL TEAM: 1967

SOUTH

Name	School	Pos.	Ht.	Wt.
Mark Box	Altus	E	6-2	205
Marco DeGulsti	OC McGuinness	E-FB	6-1	205
Bruce Deloney	OC Douglass	E	6-6	215
Larry Gallmore	McAlester	T	6-0	200
Albert Garrett	Tuttle	T	6-2	185
John Hinson	Midwest City	T	5-11	205
Robert Jenson	Yukon	T-FB	6-5	225
Mike Laub	El Reno	T	6-0	200
Lindy Pearson	Putnam City	T	6-4	210
Paul Riley	Marietta	T	6-2	202
Charles Zink	OC Northeast	T	6-0	200
Randy Brown	Norman	G	5-10	200
Larry Newton	Eufaula	G	6-0	190
LeRoy Taylor	Duncan	C	6-1	220
Rex Blankenship	Spiro	QB	6-1	180
Ronnie Duke	Carnegie	QB	5-11	168
Mike Jones	Crooked Oak	QB	5-11	170
Rick Worley	Putnam City	QB	6-2	180
Roy Bell	Clinton	HB	6-0	195
Jim Calip	Hobart	HB	5-11	185
Walter Ganaway	Lone Wolf	HB	5-11	180
Chip Land	Midwest City	HB	5-10	165
Bill Robey	Lawton	HB	5-10	180
Larry Colbert	Duncan	FB-HB	6-1	192
Lindell Shoemake	Lindsay	FB	6-0	205

OKLAHOMA ALL-STATE FOOTBALL TEAM: 1968

NORTH

Name	School	Pos.	Ht.	Wt.
Steve Fry	Blackwell	E	6-3	198
Roger Hilton	Beaver	E	6-3	200
Mike McLaughlin	Cherokee	E	6-5	205
Alan Totten	Chandler	E	6-3	185
Neil Acker	Okmulgee	T	6-2	210
Ernie Harris	Tulsa Central	T	6-1	245
John Markert	Stroud	T	6-2	230
Ron Revard	Tulsa Kelley	T-FB	6-2	210
Hugh Vertrees	Sperry	T	6-0	215
Duke Atterberry	Pawhuska	G	6-0	195
Mike Eddy	Tulsa Hale	G	6-0	215
Bill McComas	Guthrie	G	6-0	205
Don Senter	Tulsa Washington	C	5-11	188
Larry Roach	Watonga	QB	5-11	170
Rod Warner	Stillwater	QB-HB	5-11	165
Steve Williams	Collinsville	QB	5-9	160
Dick Coates	Ponca City	HB	6-1	173
David Gleason	Choctaw	HB	6-1	185
Robert Walton	Dewey	HB	5-7	167
Gordon Williams	Enid	HB	5-10	170
Thomas Zackery	Tulsa Washington	HB	5-9	172
Paul Hudson	Hominy	FB	6-2	210
Bill Orendorff	Sallisaw	FB	6-1	210
Mike Spicer	Grove	FB	5-10	185
Tommy Woods	Tulsa Hale	FB	5-10	185

OKLAHOMA ALL-STATE FOOTBALL TEAM: 1968

SOUTH

Name	School	Pos.	Ht.	Wt.
John Allen	Velma-Alma	E	6-4	210
Mark Grimes	OC Northwest	E	6-2	215
Mike Struck	Clinton	E	6-3	190
Gary Rhynes	Ada	E	6-1	195
John Carter	OC Northwest	T-HB	6-0	245
Jay Cruse	Lindsay	T	6-4	220
Anthony Gaeddart	OC Capitol Hill	T	6-3	205
Danny Reed	Minco	T-FB	6-4	205
Dwight Young	Norman	T-C	6-1	220
Raymon Hamilton	OC Douglass	G	6-1	210
James Pink	Hartshorne	G	5-10	180
Richard Carney	McAlester	C	6-0	196
Tom McEtheny	Wewoka	C	6-0	215
John Walker	Tuttle	C	6-3	190
Lester Cavins	Poteau	QB	6-1	195
Stan Templeton	Weatherford	QB	6-3	180
Lee Wayne Wood	Ardmore	QB	5-11	182
Steve Dodd	Lindsay	HB	6-3	185
Rayford Clark	Hugo	HB	5-11	200
Gerald Clopp	Midwest City	HB-LB	5-9	165
Walter Rhone	McAlester	HB	6-0	155
Ted Jackson	Weleetka	FB	6-0	200
Jerry Johnson	Hobart	FB	6-2	190
Joe Shegog	Lawton	FB	5-8	180
James Williams	Clinton	FB	6-0	190

OKLAHOMA ALL-STATE FOOTBALL TEAM: 1969

NORTH

Name	School	Pos.	Ht.	Wt.
Joe Bronson	Perry	E	6-3	225
David Duncan	Thomas	E	6-3	190
Ruben Gant	Tulsa Washington	E	6-4	215
Ronnie Pope	Laverne	E	6-6	195
Tom Stremme	Tulsa Hale	E	6-2	185
George Davis	Enid	T	6-4	210
Randy Flood	Okmulgee	T	6-2	205
Mark Lundquist	Pryor	T	6-4	210
Johnny Robinson	Hominy	T	6-2	220
Louis Taylor	Stroud	T-C	6-1	209
Percy Walker	Elk City	T	6-0	215
Ray Ennis	Clinton	G	6-1	195
Robert Love	Okmulgee	G-LB	6-0	185
Brad Moore	Cushing	C	6-1	195
Brent Blackman	Tulsa Hale	QB	5-11	160
Steve Bowling	Tulsa Webster	QB	5-11	165
Jack Risdon	Edmond	QB	6-3	190
Grant Burget	Stroud	HB	6-1	180
Richard Whitaker	Muskogee Manual	HB	6-0	170
John Winesberry	Tulsa Washington	HB	6-3	185
Gary Young	Clinton	HB	6-0	175
Butch Davis	Bixby	FB-E	6-4	211
Alfred Horsechief	Pawnee	FB	6-1	196
Greg Jones	Tulsa Memorial	FB	6-1	202
Darrell Piquet	Claremore	FB	6-1	185

OKLAHOMA ALL-STATE FOOTBALL TEAM: 1969

SOUTH

Name	School	Pos.	Ht.	Wt.
John Carroll	Norman	E	6-5	186
Oscar Franklin	OC Douglass	E	6-3	215
Bob Gary	OC Northwest	E	5-10	160
Charles Roberts	Marietta	E	6-0	194
Eddie Strange	Talihina	E	6-3	210
Jerry Perkey	Hobart	T	5-11	210
Barry Price	Midwest City	T	6-1	225
Gary Rose	Shawnee	T	5-11	190
John Skelton	Broken Bow	T	6-2	202
Jim Taylor	Walters	T	6-4	200
Brad White	Rush Springs	T	6-3	215
Jerry Pickett	OC McGuinness	G	6-0	190
Lonnie Stroud	Minco	G-LB	5-11	180
Kyle Davis	Altus	C	6-3	205
Mike McCurdy	Purcell	QB	6-3	197
Darrell Porter	OC Southeast	QB	6-1	195
Billy Bob Starr	Altus	QB	5-10	160
Jimmy Edwards	OC Classen	HB	5-10	185
David Johnson	McAlister	HB	5-10	170
Johnny Johnson	Midwest City	HB	5-10	175
Larry Marlow	Tuttle	HB	5-10	170
Clyde Powers	Lawton	HB	6-0	175
Billy Sanders	Putnam City	HB	5-7	160
Alan Cheatwood	Harrah	FB	6-0	180
Lucious Selman	Eufaula	FB	6-1	210

OKLAHOMA ALL–STATE FOOTBALL TEAM: 1970

NORTH

Name	School	Pos.	Ht.	Wt.
Rick Gambrell	Tulsa Memorial	E	6-5	215
Brian Hamar	Thomas	E	6-0	170
Jess Hudson	Hominy	E	6-1	210
Bob Crowder	Chandler	T	6-3	240
Mike Fanning	Tulsa Edison	T	6-7	232
Brad Hutchison	Enid	T	6-1	225
Mike Jones	Nowata	T	6-3	250
Bruce Neph	Stillwater	T-C	6-3	220
Mark McMinn	Buffalo	G	5-11	200
Terry Webb	Muskogee	G	6-1	198
Bob Lorenz	Clinton	C	6-2	180
Ron Pittman	Watonga	C	6-1	205
Mark Schatz	Tonkawa	C	6-3	195
Clyde Crutchmer	Okmulgee	QB	6-0	170
E. N. Simon	Clinton	QB	6-0	185
James Sykora	Stroud	QB	6-2	185
Jeff Troutt	Helena	QB	6-3	190
Kevin Vietti	Pryor	QB	6-4	195
Mike Bollenbach	Kingfisher	HB	6-1	195
Mike Heath	Okmulgee	HB	5-11	180
Randy Hughes	Tulsa Memorial	HB	6-5	195
Jim Melot	Edmond	HB	5-11	189
Gary Barnoskie	Vian	FB	6-0	190
Danny McClure	Elk City	FB	6-0	205
George Palmer	El Reno	FB	6-0	210

OKLAHOMA ALL-STATE FOOTBALL TEAM: 1970

SOUTH

Name	School	Pos.	Ht.	Wt.
Ron Boyer	Putnam City	E	6-3	200
Gerald Kidd	OC John Marshall	E	5-11	175
Euell Pope	Lawton	E	6-3	210
Jim Roper	Shawnee	E	6-3	215
Jerry Arnold	Putnam West	T	6-2	200
Glynn Browning	Yukon	T	6-0	210
Mike Flesher	Lindsay	T	6-4	245
Richard Mims	Lawton Eisenhower	T	5-11	200
L. C. Stewart	Altus	T	6-3	220
Russ Tribble	Midwest City	T	6-4	230
Scott Brunner	Wetumka	G	6-1	190
Tommy Sparkman	Anadarko	G	5-11	191
Dennis Buchanan	OC Southeast	C	6-3	210
Steve Davis	Sallisaw	QB	6-1	180
Jim Evans	Durant	QB	6-0	180
Gary Vorpahl	Duncan	QB	6-1	180
Freddie Carolina	OC Classen	HB	5-10	170
Edward Gholson	Lawton	HB	5-10	165
Steve Harris	OC Northwest	HB	6-1	198
Darrell Paden	Hartshorne	HB	5-11	185
Mark Richard	Minco	HB	6-1	185
Mike Terry	Lindsay	HB	6-0	175
Duard Thomas	Ada	HB	6-1	190
Bob Suellentrop	Midwest City	FB	5-10	190
Jamie Thomas	Ada	FB	6-2	220

OKLAHOMA ALL-STATE FOOTBALL TEAM: 1971

NORTH

Name	School	Pos.	Ht.	Wt.
Chuck Goodner	Texhoma	E	6-3	195
Doyle Green	Tahlequah	E	6-1	170
Wes Nimmo	Ponca City	E	6-3	210
Brent West	Chandler	E	6-2	165
Joe Cannon	Broken Arrow	T	6-2	210
Ray Jefferson	Tulsa Washington	T	6-3	195
Mitch McGehee	Jenks	T	6-2	195
Wade Moseley	Watonga	T	6-0	225
Jimbo Elrod	Tulsa East Central	G	6-1	203
Steve Lloyd	Perry	G	5-11	208
Jim Bob Richard	Buffalo	C-T	6-4	240
Allen Roberts	Miami	C-T	6-2	207
Sylvester Berry	Tulsa Washington	QB	6-1	170
Rodney Kilgore	Tulsa Webster	QB-HB	5-11	170
Larry Briggs	Vian	HB	5-11	180
Kenny Crosswhite	Hennessey	HB	6-1	175
Milton Curry	Watonga	HB	6-0	170
Butch Hill	El Reno	HB	5-10	165
Ken Langston	Fairland	HB	6-0	205
Bill Littrell	Muskogee	HB	6-0	198
Dewey McClain	Okmulgee	HB	6-4	195
Tinker Owens	Miami	HB	6-1	165
Sam Ryan	Okeene	FB	6-2	215
Jim Stone	Stroud	FB	6-2	190
Lonnie Wright	Choctaw	FB	6-3	235

OKLAHOMA ALL-STATE FOOTBALL TEAM: 1971

SOUTH

Name	School	Pos.	Ht.	Wt.
Randy Bass	Lawton	E	6-3	195
Ron Downing	Ardmore	E	6-1	185
David Durbin	Atoka	E	5-9	150
Ralph Kulbyth	Marlow	E	6-6	221
David Lawyer	Seminole	T	6-1	230
Brent Price	Midwest City	T	6-1	235
Dewey Selmon	Eufaula	T-HB	6-2	240
Leroy Selmon	Eufaula	T-FB	6-3	255
David Ellis	OC Southeast	G	6-0	215
Dee Hines	Tuttle	G	6-1	200
Kyle Lackey	Lindsay	G	6-1	185
Robert Baker	Seminole	C	6-2	220
Tony Brantley	Putnam City	QB	6-0	195
Coy Everett	Shawnee	QB	6-2	175
Robin Ameen	Midwest City	HB	5-7	150
Mike Barbour	Comanche	HB	6-1	220
Joe Boley	Altus	HB	5-11	180
Billy Daniels	Lawton MacArthur	HB	6-0	205
Nolan Franklin	Lawton Eisenhower	HB	5-10	175
Billy Keith Gray	Ada	HB	5-8	165
Chuck Henson	Shawnee	HB	5-11	175
Henry McGowan	Grandfield	HB	6-4	223
Randy Coffman	Altus	FB	6-1	205
Ron Few	Stigler	FB	6-1	200
C. J. Peachlyn	Pauls Valley	FB	6-1	190

OKLAHOMA ALL-STATE FOOTBALL TEAM: 1972

NORTH

Name	School	Pos.	Ht.	Wt.
Steve Elliott	Tahequah	E	6-2	175
Carl Stremme	Tulsa Hale	E	6-1	185
Kevin Brooks	El Reno	T	6-0	205
David Cook	Davenport	T	6-2	230
Allen Rosenberg	Vian	T	6-1	225
Kenneth Snell	Choctaw	T	6-3	245
Ron Gilliam	Tulsa Washington	G	6-2	205
Rodney Miles	Okeene	G	6-3	215
Scott Warden	Tulsa Central	C	6-1	205
Marvin Ellis	Okmulgee	LB	6-1	200
Greg Murfin	Stroud	LB	6-2	215
Ross Murphy	Tulsa Memorial	LB	6-4	220
Doug Johnson	Ponca City	QB	5-10	160
Mike McVay	Beaver	QB	6-1	198
Bob Womack	Claremore	QB	5-11	175
Rick Butler	Hominy	HB	5-11	170
Les Divens	Tulsa East Central	HB	6-0	203
Wayne Jones	Elk City	HB	6-1	190
Bobby Miller	Edmond	HB	6-2	185
R. L. Pittman	Watonga	HB	5-10	165
Steve Ramsey	Tulsa Hale	HB	5-10	180
John Winchester	Texhoma	HB	5-11	180
Gerald McMullin	Kingfisher	FB	6-0	188
Artie Puckett	Sayre	FB	6-0	180
Gary Reamey	Owasso	FB	5-11	180

OKLAHOMA ALL-STATE FOOTBALL TEAM: 1972

SOUTH

Name	School	Pos.	Ht.	Wt.
Danny Hall	Midwest City	E	6-3	185
Sam Lisle	Putnam City	E	6-1	190
Rick Magee	OC Southeast	E	5-10	185
John Boyer	Putnam City	T	6-2	225
Chez Evans	Seminole	T	6-3	275
Jay Holman	Altus	T	6-2	225
Jim Ledford	OC Grant	T	6-2	220
David Orr	Lindsay	T	6-4	222
Arthur Foss	Lawton MacArthur	G	6-0	205
Jamie Melendez	Lawton	G	6-2	225
Mike Smith	Lawton Eisenhower	C	6-3	225
Bill Dalke	Hobart	LB	6-1	210
Joe Storey	Broken Arrow	LB	6-1	208
Joe Avanzini	Coalgate	QB	6-2	180
Jim Derrick	Checotah	QB	6-2	195
Joe Reynolds	Purcell	QB	6-2	185
Eddie Porter	OC Southeast	QB	5-11	180
Bill Whiteley	Lawton	QB	6-0	175
Jesse Cohee	Lawton Eisenhower	HB	5-10	175
David James	Pauls Valley	HB	6-0	170
Greg Petree	Shawnee	HB	6-0	170
Tim Tinneman	Yukon	HB	6-2	190
Mark Bane	Sallisaw	FB	6-3	200
Don Erwin	Healdton	FB	5-11	210
Paul Sturdivant	Moore	FB	6-1	200

OKLAHOMA ALL-STATE FOOTBALL TEAM: 1973

NORTH

Name	School	Pos.	Ht.	Wt.
Phil Davis	Tulsa Hale	E	6-1	210
Ronnie Jones	Okmulgee	E	6-0	175
Reginal Midget	Tulsa Washington	E	6-1	170
John Beasley	Sapulpa	T	6-4	215
San Claphan	Stilwell	T	6-6	240
Harvey Johnson	Tulsa Central	T	6-5	215
James Norton	Davenport	T	6-3	205
Roy Jones	Owasso	G	6-3	235
J. D. Parkerson	Skiatook	G	5-11	195
Jon Myers	Miami	C	6-1	190
Melvin Barrens	Tulsa Washington	QB	6-1	170
Ken Burgess	Bartlesville College	QB	6-0	175
Steve Miller	Tulsa Hale	QB	5-11	170
Louis Patman	Crescent	QB	6-0	180
Kyle Phillips	Woodward	QB	6-1	180
Bob Walker	Vinita	QB	5-11	178
Aaron Crawford	Hominy	HB	6-0	170
Wes Hankins	Bristow	HB	5-10	170
Billy Lynn	Elk City	HB	5-11	165
Leslie Smith	Kingfisher	HB	5-9	162
L. C. Taylor	Prague	HB	5-11	170
Steve Ross	Edmond	FB	5-10	185
Stan Young	Buffalo	FB	6-0	220
Danny Clark	Tulsa Webster	LB	6-2	190
Randy Halliburton	Laverne	LB	5-10	168

OKLAHOMA ALL-STATE FOOTBALL TEAM: 1973

SOUTH

Name	School	Pos.	Ht.	Wt.
Stanford Cherry	Tuttle	E	6-3	220
Chico Phillips	Healdton	E	6-1	215
Ricky Roach	Shawnee	E	5-10	150
Forest Bradley	OC McGuinness	T	6-6	215
Jody Farthing	Midwest City	T	6-0	228
Mike Hawkins	Shawnee	T	6-1	235
Dorian Jared	Carnegie	T	6-4	200
Jeff Ward	Moore	T	6-6	260
Steve McCord	Comanche	G	6-0	221
Vance Sharpe	Putnam City	G	5-10	220
Albert Walz	Lawton	C	6-0	220
Dean Blevins	Norman	QB	6-0	180
Jeff Brown	OC Classen	HB	5-11	180
John Bunch	Spiro	HB	6-1	185
Ralph Cubit	Broken Arrow	HB	5-11	197
Vaughn Lusby	Lawton MacArthur	HB	5-9	175
Phil Maggard	Broken Bow	HB	6-0	175
Jackie Schuman	Putnam City	HB	5-7	155
Myron Shoate	Spiro	HB	5-11	185
Bobby Simonton	Lindsay	HB	6-2	192
David Campbell	Wynnewood	FB	5-10	192
Allen Grieb	OC Northeast	FB	6-1	190
Larry Moore	OC Southeast	FB	6-0	190
Kevin Hayes	Putnam West	LB	5-7	176
Clifford Thrift	Purcell	LB	6-2	197

OKLAHOMA ALL-STATE FOOTBALL TEAM: 1974

NORTH

Name	School	Pos.	Ht.	Wt.
Steve Hesser	Sillwater	E	6-1	185
Darryl Jones	OC Millwood	E	6-0	160
Barry Bales	Enid	T	6-3	230
Robert Hardy	Tulsa Washington	T	6-1	240
Tim Luman	Choctaw	T	6-5	210
Phil Scott	Sperry	T	6-3	212
Earl Stripling	Tulsa Washington	T	6-1	240
Terry Upton	Tulsa Kelley	T	6-3	220
Neil Ramsey	Tulsa Hale	G	6-0	205
Ken Hargrove	Jenks	C	6-2	205
Kenny McKosato	Perkins	QB	6-0	165
Steve Mixon	Stroud	QB	6-2	180
David Rader	Tulsa Rogers	QB	6-3	207
David Watkins	Catoosa	QB	5-9	175
Marc Brumble	Tulsa Hale	HB	5-9	170
Gaylon Cox	Okeene	HB	6-1	180
Bennie McCracken	Owasso	HB	5-9	170
Jack Taylor	Skiatook	HB	6-0	170
Brad Bates	Pryor	FB	6-2	190
Mike Gaither	Tulsa Memorial	FB	6-3	220
Dale Hubbard	Elk City	FB	6-1	195
Bruce Terronez	Davenport	FB	6-2	215
Audie Eversole	Cushing	NG	6-2	205
Jeff Bitsko	Sand Springs	LB	6-0	190
Mike Dean	Hominy	LB	6-2	185

OKLAHOMA ALL-STATE FOOTBALL TEAM: 1974

SOUTH

Name	School	Pos.	Ht.	Wt.
Dale Burch	Idabel	E	6-4	160
John Cobbs	Del City	E	6-3	210
John Cherry	Putnam West	T	6-3	215
Larry Jackson	Lawton MacArthur	T	6-1	215
Gene MCIntyre	Lawton Eisenhower	T	6-3	225
Mark Rawlings	Putnam City	T	6-3	230
John Walker	Altus	T	6-0	220
Guy Sewell	Atoka	G	6-1	205
Randy Weeaks	Comanche	G	6-2	218
Clifford Agee	Sulphur	QB	6-1	205
Mark Greene	Tuttle	QB	6-3	210
Dewayne Harrell	Pernell	QB	6-0	175
Joe Hough	Putnam City	QB	6-0	195
Gregg Byram	Norman	HB	6-3	180
Gerald Green	Purcell	HB	5-11	170
Lee High	OC John Marshall	HB	5-10	170
Chipp Latham	Rush Springs	HB	6-2	190
Darnell Scott	Spiro	HB	6-1	185
Roy Smth	Wynnewood	HB	6-0	175
Jesse Cross	Lawton	FB	5-11	172
Jeff Jesse	Midwest City	FB	6-0	205
Chris Reynolds	Shawnee	FB	6-1	180
Mark Perrault	OC McGuinness	LB	6-1	223
Chuck Roberts	Ada	S	6-3	180
Sherwood Taylor	Ada	S	6-2	185

OKLAHOMA ALL-STATE FOOTBALL TEAM: 1975

NORTH

Name	School	Pos.	Ht.	Wt.
Johnny Scott	Fairfax	SE	6-2	168
Jerry Greenwood	Bristow	TE	6-3	195
Terry Jones	Roland	TE	6-3	240
Pat Nault	Okeene	TE	6-3	195
Keith Cain	Tulsa McLain	T	6-2	220
Jin Carner	Tulsa Hale	T	6-4	255
Tim Clancy	Tulsa Kelley	T	6-0	205
Jim Colvard	Jenks	T	6-3	218
Ed Culver	Tahlequah	T	6-4	265
Mike Schwager	Stillwater	T	6-3	217
Terry Vincent	Fairland	T	6-6	235
Rex Ross	Miami	G	6-2	195
Steve Nicholson	Tulsa Memorial	G	6-2	215
Bret Fyffe	Okmulgee	C	6-2	210
Keith Schneider	Woodward	QB	6-0	165
Jeff Swab	Tulsa Cascia Hall	QB	6-1	190
Bruce Taton	Tulsa Hale	QB	6-3	210
Mark Wackenhuth	Tulsa Mason	QB	6-1	190
John Austin	Beggs	HB	5-11	175
Barry Burget	Stroud	HB	6-3	205
Mike Green	Pawnee	HB	6-0	180
R. C. Morrow	Okmulgee	HB	5-8	165
Brent Payne	Sperry	HB	5-10	170
Dan Keith	Owasso	FB	6-1	205
David Knight	Tulsa Washington	LB	6-0	190

OKLAHOMA ALL-STATE FOOTBALL TEAM: 1975

SOUTH

Name	School	Pos.	Ht.	Wt.
Ken McNeil	Spiro	SE	6-0	170
Ben Fruehauf	Midwest City	TE	6-4	210
Bill Nowlin	Sallisaw	TE	6-4	220
Jeff Couch	Cordell	T	6-4	217
Riley Goodin	Mustang	T	6-2	233
Art Johnson	Lawton Eisenower	T	6-4	235
Gary Morgan	Duncan	T	6-0	230
Todd Ranger	Putnam City	T	6-3	255
Joe Walstad	Altus	T	6-4	250
Randy Wilson	Del City	T	6-0	220
Greg Loman	Pauls Valley	G	6-0	235
Ronnie Wilson	Blanchard	G	6-0	190
Syd Haynes	OC Grant	C	6-4	245
Ricky Bowens	Chickasha	QB	5-8	140
Scott Burger	Putnam West	QB	6-2	190
Ricky Dorman	Lindsay	QB	5-10	175
J. C. Watts	Eufaula	QB	6-0	205
Jimmy Allen	Idabel	HB	6-0	190
Paul Ameen	Midwest City	HB	6-0	185
Terry Faulkner	Hartshorne	HB	6-1	187
Freddie Hurd	Ardmore	HB	5-8	168
Steve Jones	Clinton	FB	5-11	190
Jay Jordan	OC Southeast	NG	5-11	188
Mike Berry	OC Millwood	LB	6-2	190
Chuck Williams	Norman	LB	5-11	180

OKLAHOMA ALL-STATE FOOTBALL TEAM: 1976

NORTH

Name	School	Pos.	Ht.	Wt.
Randy Nelson	Woodward	SE	6-2	175
Jim Jones	Turpin	TE	6-5	220
Ernie Caruthers	Owasso	T	6-3	210
Ed Johnson	Bixby	T	6-1	240
Richard Turner	Edmond	T	6-3	240
Doug Wyer	Jenks	T	6-3	220
Donnie Oates	Tulsa Washington	G	6-4	220
Bobby Irvin	Beggs	NG	6-0	195
Jerry Ross	Tulsa Memorial	NG	5-10	195
Bart Latham	Bristow	C	6-4	260
Tom Schneider	Thomas	C	6-2	220
Russ Henderson	Vinita	QB	6-2	175
Jeff Jones	Crescent	QB	5-6	145
Tim McSperitt	Watonga	QB	6-1	190
Steve Whaley	Cleveland	QB	6-4	180
Arthur Crosby	Fairfax	HB	5-10	175
Mike Field	Stillwater	HB	6-0	185
Jamie Haines	Catoosa	HB	5-9	165
Steve Jarboe	Pryor	HB	6-0	190
Mark Olbert	Edmond	HB	5-11	190
Vincent Orange	Tulsa Webster	HB	5-8	200
Eugene Simmons	Muskogee	HB	6-1	190
Steve Tate	Luther	HB	6-1	185
Brad Smith	Miami	FB	6-0	195
Mike Coast	Bartlesville Sooner	LB	6-1	200

OKLAHOMA ALL-STATE FOOTBALL TEAM: 1976

SOUTH

Name	School	Pos.	Ht.	Wt.
Rory O'Neal	Seminole	SE	5-10	170
Bruce Jones	Lindsay	TE	6-5	200
Curtis Boone	Lawton MacAuthur	T	6-3	235
Wes Conaster	Ardmore	T	6-3	245
Scott Dawson	Shawnee	T	6-2	240
Roy Hackett	Midwest City	T	6-5	230
George Madden	OC Douglass	T	5-10	220
Frank Moore	OC Millwood	T	6-6	235
Steve Trimble	Moore	T	6-3	230
Jeff Sheckles	Yukon	G	6-1	220
John Connor	Tuttle	C	6-3	200
Dan Hammond	Duncan	C	6-1	180
Sherwood Anderson	Okemah	QB	5-11	175
Tom Bradley	Pauls Valley	QB	6-1	185
Jay Jimerson	Norman	QB	5-10	170
Eric Anderson	McAlester	HB	5-5	150
Bruce Compton	Norman	HB	6-2	185
Brent Hagar	Ada	HB	5-9	160
Steven Hammond	Del City	HB	5-11	195
Byron Paul	Altus	HB	6-2	180
Mark Powers	Putnam West	HB	5-10	185
Clifford Chatman	Clinton	FB	6-2	210
Ken Oleson	Del City	FB	6-2	190
John Higginbotham	Hugo	LB	6-2	235
Jeff McKinney	Putnam West	LB	6-1	210

OKLAHOMA ALL-STATE FOOTBALL TEAM: 1977

NORTH

Name	School	Pos.	Ht.	Wt.
Kelly Beesley	Bristow	SE	6-2	185
Zack Webster	Stillwater	SE	6-0	170
Kevin Stringfellow	Bixby	TE	6-1	185
Doug Freeman	Collinsville	T	6-1	230
Dan Hoover	Muskogee	T	6-3	225
Clay Loosen	Watonga	T	6-3	210
Robin Patterson	Clinton	T	6-3	225
Jody Tillman	Fairfax	T	6-5	235
Steve Vallon	Owasso	T	6-3	245
Larry Cooper	Ft. Gibson	G	6-2	225
Davis Wilson	Sand Springs	G	6-2	212
Kevin Ormand	Ponca City	C	6-8	228
Charles Davis	Tulsa Washington	QB	6-0	195
Bobby Grayson	Beggs	QB	6-0	170
Craig Lance	Fairfax	QB	5-11	175
Gary Johnson	Watonga	QB	5-11	170
Randy Jones	Crescent	HB	5-11	180
Dale Nauit	Okeene	HB	6-1	175
Jay Sturgeon	Claremore	HB	6-3	193
Rodney Tate	Beggs	HB	6-0	175
Mike Swart	Kingfisher	FB	6-0	210
Cecil Beisel	Perry	LB	6-1	210
Jim Galbraith	Tahlequah	LB	6-3	205
Brett Brownlee	Hennessey	DB	6-3	182
Randy Rawlinson	Tulsa East Central	DB	6-5	200

OKLAHOMA ALL-STATE FOOTBALL TEAM: 1977

SOUTH

Name	School	Pos.	Ht.	Wt.
Al Kilgore	Altus	SE	6-2	170
Brian Butler	Ada	TE	6-1	190
Steve Holmes	Yukon	TE	6-4	232
Bill Bajema	Norman	T	6-5	220
Ed Branch	Davis	T	6-3	260
Derwin Cantley	Broken Bow	T	6-1	245
Jim Hile	Seminole	T	6-2	215
Chris Kinniard	Comanche	T	6-2	218
Kelly Mitchell	Sallisaw	T	6-4	228
Ken Muncy	Shawnee	T	6-5	245
Bruce Scott	OC Western Heights	T	6-2	245
Bob Shaff	Putnam City	T	6-2	225
King White	Poteau	T	6-1	230
Jackie Autry	Blanchard	C	6-2	200
Cary Jones	Duncan	QB	5-10	165
Smokey McCarthey	Del City	QB	6-1	190
Randy Page	OC Southeast	QB	6-0	170
Kelly Phelps	Putnam City	QB	5-11	185
Scott Tinaley	Putnam West	QB	6-2	185
Andy Boyd	Fox	HB	5-11	187
Jerry Lewis	Spiro	HB	6-0	180
Venoy Shields	Atoka	HB	5-9	170
Terry Suellentrop	Midwest City	FB	5-11	190
Wayne Carden	Lawton Eisenhower	LB	5-11	187
Joe Keith Foster	Lindsay	LB	5-10	190

OKLAHOMA ALL-STATE FOOTBALL TEAM: 1978

NORTH

Name	School	Pos.	Ht.	Wt.
Mark Cromer	Broken Arrow	SE	6-1	175
Steve Dunlap	Thomas	SE-QB	6-0	168
Brian Henderson	Sapulpa	TE-MG	6-1	217
Terry Clark	Tulsa Kelley	T	6-2	226
Don Franks	Watonga	T-DG	6-0	230
Paul Lamie	Okeene	T	6-3	240
Jim Northcutt	Tulsa Mason	T	6-6	241
Paul Parker	Tulsa Washington	T	6-4	280
Tony Simek	Prague	T	6-3	240
Mike Wimmer	Muskogee	G-LB	5-11	190
Ron Whitely	Edmond	C	6-4	220
Daryl Wiesman	Tulsa Hale	C-DT	6-1	185
Aaron Carpenter	Collinsville	QB	6-2	180
Reuben Jones	Tulsa McLain	QB	6-2	195
Dwyane Downing	Vinita	QB	6-1	185
Greg Johnson	Watonga	QB-DB	5-10	175
Dannye Webb	Ponca City	QB-DB	6-0	168
Beany Alexander	Tulsa McLain	HB	6-2	185
Rocky Hunter	Guymon	HB	5-10	180
Steve Pollard	Newkirk	HB	5-8	173
Brett White	Jenks	HB	6-1	195
John Blake	Sand Springs	FB-HG	6-0	240
Ed Desherow	Edmond	LB	6-3	220
Doug Furnas	Commerce	LB	5-11	210
Juan James	Okmulgee	DB	6-2	180

OKLAHOMA ALL-STATE FOOTBALL TEAM: 1978

SOUTH

Name	School	Pos.	Ht.	Wt.
Keith Estes	Henryetta	SE	6-1	185
Dan Neely	Poteau	SE	6-1	175
Kenny Sutton	Duncan	TE-LB	6-0	185
Jerry Thorne	Lawton MacAuthur	DE	6-0	175
Mike Ballard	Putnam West	T	6-3	205
John Brentlinger	Midwest City	T	6-4	220
Bill Green	Duncan	T	5-11	230
Glenn Hill	Atoka	T	6-2	225
Steve Hogue	Ada	T	6-2	225
David Pearson	Putnam City	T	6-2	220
Robert Schwab	OC Western Heights	T	6-3	235
Kevin Boyd	Fox	G-LB	6-1	215
Gary Lewis	OC Millwood	G-DT	6-4	220
Shan Kirtley	Sulphur	C-LB	6-0	203
Wes Stone	Purcell	C-DT	6-1	230
Allen Rock	Clinton	QB	6-0	175
Bobby Shannon	Marlow	QB	5-9	165
Stan Fixico	Konawa	QB-DB	5-10	165
Lorenzo Breath	Fox	HB	5-11	181
Wayne Ellenberg	MWC Carl Albert	HB	6-1	190
Curtis Jones	Lawton	HB	5-10	165
Steve McKeaver	Altus	HB	6-1	195
Steve Mooney	Putnam West	HB	5-9	160
Paul Smith	Durant	HB	6-0	188
Kirk Phillips	Spiro	HB-LB	6-2	190

OKLAHOMA ALL-STATE FOOTBALL TEAM: 1979

NORTH

Name	School	Pos.	Ht.	Wt..
Jim Evans	Tulsa Washington	SE	5-9	158
Ricky Bryan	Coweta	TE	6-5	230
Kevin Harlan	Ponca City	TE	6-3	214
Brent Burks	Oologah	T	6-7	235
David Hicks	Tulsa Memorial	T	6-6	230
Rodney Maynard	Laverne	T	6-1	216
David Dillingham	Jenks	C	6-5	225
Brian Vosburgh	Tulsa Kelley	G	6-3	210
Kent Mutzig	Tahlequah	NG	6-1	195
Scott Newland	Jenks	DE	6-2	195
Duayne Deaver	Perkins	QB	6-2	190
Billy McClure	Crescent	QB	5-10	165
Bobby Biskup	Tulsa Hale	B	6-0	185
Jeryl Jennings	Guthrie	B	6-0	185
Kelly Keith	Collinsville	B	5-9	165
Kenny Kinnard	Claremore	B	6-3	187
Jerome Ledbetter	Muskogee	B	5-11	195
Chuck Mitchell	Okmulgee	B	5-11	205
Matt Monger	Miami	B	6-2	190
David VanCleave	Kingfisher	B	5-9	150
Monty Dossman	Pryor	LB	6-0	220
Kelly Goode	Tulsa Hale	LB	6-1	211
Rocky Jefferson	Clinton	LB	6-3	205
Jeff Leiding	Tulsa Union	LB	6-4	234
Jack Shipp	Stillwater	LB	6-3	200

OKLAHOMA ALL-STATE FOOTBALL TEAM: 1979

SOUTH

Name	School	Pos.	Ht.	Wt.
James Carter	Durant	TE	6-3	190
Chris Edgemon	Davis	TE	6-2	205
Tim Randolph	Midwest City	TE	6-4	235
Paul Bryant	Durant	T	6-1	237
Lloyd London	McAlester	T	5-11	245
Eric Pope	Seminole	T	6-2	255
Brad Rollow	Putnam West	T	6-3	238
Garky Schornick	Duncan	T	6-4	220
Terry Summers	Ada	T	6-3	235
Mac Alexander	Chickasha	G	6-1	240
Ricky Oliver	Midwest City	G	6-1	210
Justin Jackson	Tuttle	C	6-0	205
George Schutz	Lawton	DE	6-0	200
Curtis Cain	Putnam North	QB	6-3	205
Brent Dennis	Blanchard	QB	5-9	190
Kyle Duke	Putnam West	QB	6-0	200
Kent Roulston	Wewoka	QB	5-10	160
Bryan Dalton	Lawton MacAuthur	B	6-0	180
Jeff Dodd	Lindsay	B	6-1	205
Mike Emery	OC Western Heights	B	5-10	175
Jimmy Don Green	Purcell	B	5-7	146
Tom Presley	Hartshorne	B	6-2	190
Thomas Benson	Ardmore	LB	6-2	210
Tom Flemons	Altus	LB	6-2	219
Joe Jordan	Blanchard	LB	6-3	210

OKLAHOMA ALL-STATE FOOTBALL TEAM: 1980

FIRST TEAM

Offense

Name	School	Position	Ht.	Wt.	Class
Randy Martin	Roland	End	6-3	210	Senior
Aaron Bruner	Davis	End	5-10	160	Senior
Clay Miller	Norman	Lineman	6-5	238	Senior
Martin Clagg	Lindsay	Lineman	6-1	220	Senior
Scott Leggett	Muskogee	Lineman	6-3	240	Senior
Vincent James	Okmulgee	Lineman	6-0	240	Senior
Jerry Petty	Newcastle	Lineman	5-10	210	Senior
Brad Calip	Hobart	Quarterback	5-10	160	Senior
Tim Blount	Sallisaw	Running Back	5-9	160	Senior
Kelly Cook	Midwest City	Running Back	5-11	195	Senior
Marvel Rogers	Carl Albert	Running Back	5-9	168	Senior
Craig Benson	Sallisaw	Specialist	5-9	168	Senior

Defense

Name	School	Position	Ht.	Wt.	Class
Steve Nicholson	Stillwater	Lineman	6-0	175	Senior
Doug Meritan	Tulsa Memorial	Lineman	6-2	215	Senior
Phil Jones	Putnam City	Lineman	6-2	195	Senior
Lee Bob Martin	Morris	Lineman	6-1	220	Senior
Phil Wilson	Putnam West	Linebacker	6-1	195	Senior
Toby Daugherty	Mustang	Linebacker	6-2	230	Senior
Brian Man	Stilwell	Linebacker	5-11	205	Senior
Greg Hinkle	Lindsay	Linebacker	5-10	205	Senior
John Cooper	Tulsa Memorial	Back	6-1	180	Senior
Tim Gibbs	Bixby	Back	6-2	170	Senior
Mark Bilby	Jenks	Back	6-2	185	Senior

OKLAHOMA ALL-STATE FOOTBALL TEAM: 1980

SECOND TEAM

Offense

Name	School	Position	Ht.	Wt.	Class
Chris Hauhuth	Heritage Hall	End	6-3	190	Senior
Andy Barron	Star Spencer	End	6-6	200	Senior
Paul Hammond	Clinton	Lineman	6-2	245	Senior
Paul Ferrer	Midwest City	Lineman	6-4	230	Senior
Bo Cotton	Bristow	Lineman	6-6	250	Senior
Blake Tucker	Stillwater	Lineman	6-0	200	Senior
Greg Nichols	Durant	Lineman	6-2	252	Senior
Joe Don Litsch	Thomas	Quarterback	5-11	188	Senior
Eddie Goodlow	Altus	Running Back	5-11	195	Senior
Bryant Calip	Hobart	Running Back	6-0	175	Senior
Bobby Wright	Vian	Running Back	5-10	187	Senior

Defense

Name	School	Position	Ht.	Wt.	Class
Terry Casillas	Tulsa E. Central	Lineman	6-3	245	Senior
Dale Lewis	Midwest City	Lineman	6-2	240	Senior
Anthony Nibs	Carl Albert	Lineman	6-5	225	Senior
Paul Smith	Sperry	Lineman	6-4	240	Senior
Brian Brunner	T. Washington	Lineman	6-3	230	Senior
Bill Byford	Chisholm	Linebacker	6-3	215	Senior
Wink Kopczynski	Ada	Linebacker	6-0	195	Senior
Tony Damron	Kingston	Linebacker	6-0	195	Senior
Rodney Douglas	Lawton	Back	5-11	193	Senior
Lynn Beck	Blanchard	Back	6-3	170	Senior
Charles Crawford	Hominy	Back	6-1	196	Senior

OKLAHOMA ALL-STATE FOOTBALL TEAM: 1981

FIRST TEAM

Offense

Name	School	Position
Jimmy Long	Midwest City	Wide Receiver
Phil Cole	Marlow	Wide Receiver
Craig Vosburgh	Tulsa Kelly	Tight End
David Alexander	Broken Arrow	Lineman
Kirt Billen	Newcastle	Lineman
Alex Darrow	Skistook	Lineman
Tony Duplisse	Putnam North	Lineman
David Jones	Claremore	Lineman
Ronnie Waskiewicz	Lawton Eisenhower	Quarterback
Steve Looper	Cordell	Quarterback
Eddie Boyd	Cushing	Running Back
Mike Cutter	Putnam West	Running Back
Spencer Tillman	Tulsa Edison	Running Back

Defense

Name	School	Position
Dale Drew	Del City	Lineman
Keith Hess	Lawton	Lineman
Ernie Fisher	Tulsa Union	Lineman
Jeff Volz	Collinsville	Lineman
Jeff Thornbrue	McLoud	Lineman
Brent Johnson	Stillwater	Linebacker
Mike Mantie	Miami	Linebacker
Dennis Mattheyer	Stroud	Linebacker
Richard Marler	Oaks	Back
Neil Sharum	Sallisaw	Back
Kevin Andrews	Tulsa Kelley	Back
Chris Meyer	Edmond	Back
Ed Hawkins	Okeene	Specialist

OKLAHOMA ALL-STATE FOOTBALL TEAM: 1981

SECOND TEAM

Offense

Name	School	Position
Mark Mitchell	Hobart	Wide Receiver
Rick Smith	Sallisaw	Wide Receiver
Matt Salyer	Stroud	Tight End
Russ Corbin	Newcastle	Lineman
Mark Galbraith	Tahlequah	Lineman
Sid Niles	Enid	Lineman
Sam Woodfork	Seminole	Lineman
John Ward	Talihina	Lineman
Brian Hulsey	Tuttle	Quarterback
Mark Bliss	Medford	Quarterback
Lyndel Gibson	Newcastle	Running Back
Barry Nault	Okeene	Running Back
John Wright	Wynnewood	Running Back

Defense

Name	School	Position
Mark Clark	Lawton Eisenhower	Lineman
Greg Strope	Tulsa East Central	Lineman
Clifford Burney	Lawton MacArthur	Lineman
Robert Willard	Ada	Lineman
Keith Skelton	Sallisaw	Lineman
Scott Collingwood	Owasso	Linebacker
Edmond Pickens	Del City	Linebacker
Todd Bullock	Tulsa Union	Linebacker
Laderyl Grayson	Tulsa McLain	Back
Matt Uhr	Yukon	Back
Avery Howard	OC Grant	Back
Kyle Bayliff	Stillwater	Back
Brian Rupe	OC McGuinness	Specialist

OKLAHOMA ALL-STATE FOOTBALL TEAM: 1982

FIRST TEAM

Offense

Name	School	Position
Glynn Walker	Clinton	Quarterback
Bobby Riley	Stroud	Running Back
Henry Washington	Hobart	Running Back
Tracy Kiehl	Morris	Fullback
Chris Rainbolt	Cordell	Wide Receiver
Ty Young	Hominy	Tight End
Flint Pattison	Wewoka	Tackle
Caesar Rentie	Hartshorne	Tackle
Terry Badgewell	Dewar	Guard
Buster Glass	Kansas	Guard
Royce Scooby	OC Millwood	Center
Cliff McCain	Putnam North	Kicker
Darrin Atyia	Seminole	Punter

Defense

Name	School	Position
Mike Keil	Jenks	End
Greg Johnson	Norman	End
Tim Condrin	Jenks	Tackle
Jon Phillips	Jenks	Tackle
George Coffman	Idabel	Nose Guard
Randy Simmons	Seminole	Linebacker
Jay Richert	Clinton	Linebacker
Kerry Kincade	Wewoka	Cornerback
Todd Krehbiel	Bixby	Cornerback
Bucky Hill	El Reno	Safety
Tim Gordon	Ardmore	Safety

OKLAHOMA ALL-STATE FOOTBALL TEAM: 1982

SECOND TEAM

Offense

Name	School	Position
David Vickers	Tulsa Hale	Quarterback
Lyndel Gibson	Newcastle	Running Back
Mike Hudson	Hominy	Running Back
Kevin Brown	Ponca City	Fullback
Bruce Alcorn	Bristow	Wide Receiver
Craig Dobrinski	Okeene	Tight End
Mark Brand	Cleveland	Tackle
Chip Mitchell	Midwest City	Tackle
David Combs	Lindsay	Guard
Jay Reichenberger	Alva	Guard
Robert Young	Woodward	Center
Chris England	Fairview	Kicker
Kyle Irvin	Tulsa Union	Punter

Defense

Name	School	Position
Dean Shinault	Ponca City	End
David Van Orsdal	Bristow	End
Brad McBride	Edmond	Tackle
Terry Tumey	Tulsa Washington	Tackle
Trent Shelby	Hollis	Nose Guard
Robert Nunn	Apache	Linebacker
Scotty Wright	Vian	Linebacker
Chris McCartney	Pawhuska	Cornerback
Ronald Wright	Vian	Cornerback
Mike Rust	Stilwell	Safety
Doug Desherow	Edmond	Safety

OKLAHOMA ALL-STATE FOOTBALL TEAM: 1983

FIRST TEAM

Offense

Name	School	Position	Ht.	Wt.
Todd Hudson	Wynnewood	Quarterback	6-3	192
Lyndell Carr	Enid	Running Back	6-2	198
Patric Collins	Tulsa Washington	Running Back	5-10	180
Scott Garl	Hominy	Fullback	6-1	195
Wade Hundley	Deer Creek	Wide Receiver	6-1	160
Pat Sheehy	Purcell	Tight End	6-2	186
William Gant	Tulsa Washington	Tackle	6-2	280
Craig Satepauhoodle	Hominy	Tackle	6-4	260
Mickey Greene	OC Millwood	Guard	6-3	257
Mike Brand	Cleveland	Guard	6-4	245
Chris Stanley	Elk City	Center	6-4	220
Kelly Nemecek	Purcell	Kicker	6-0	223
Doug Robison	Putnam City	Punter	6-4	235

Defense

Name	School	Position	Ht.	Wt.
Dennis Byrd	Mustang	End	6-4	210
Scott Null	Hobart	End	5-10	175
Ron Merchberger	Morris	Tackle	6-4	210
Mike Freeman	Putman West	Tackle	6-5	225
Richard Davis	Jenks	Nose Guard	6-2	235
Steve Barth	Shattuck	Linebacker	5-11	187
Fred Burris	Broken Arrow	Linebacker	6-2	210
Jon Craig	Morris	Cornerback	6-0	176
Damon Stell	Putnam North	Cornerback	5-11	183
Logan Pendergraft	Pawhuska	Safety	5-11	185
Danny Massey	Broken Arrow	Safety	6-1	198

OKLAHOMA ALL-STATE FOOTBALL TEAM: 1983

SECOND TEAM

Offense

Name	School	Position
Vince Moore	OC Northeast	Quarterback
Don Maloney	Chickasha	Running Back
Vernell Ramsey	Broken Bow	Running Back
Lee D. Henderson	Clinton	Fullback
Bart Evans	Billings	Wide Receiver
Vic Mariano	Okmulgee	Tight End
Brad Best	Bixby	Tackle
Mike Wolfe	Miami	Tackle
Mike Barber	Midwest City	Guard
Eric Troutman	Duncan	Guard
Justin Springer	Midwest City	Center
Joey O'Donnell	Perry	Kicker
Perry Walker	Mangum	Punter

Defense

Name	School	Position
Keith Riggs	Owasso	End
Danny Collums	Enid	End
Greg Holmes	Durant	Tackle
Chris Elliot	Marlow	Tackle
Roy Reed	Durant	Nose Guard
Harry Brown	Ardmore	Linebacker
Larry Wiseley	Duncan	Linebacker
Greg Simpson	Muskogee	Cornerback
Greg Upshaw	Dewar	Cornerback
Erick Harrison	Bristow	Safety
Blly Nickles	Caddo	Safety

OKLAHOMA ALL-STATE FOOTBALL TEAM: 1984

FIRST TEAM

Offense

Name	School	Pos.	Ht.	Wt.
Terry Prichard	Moore	TE	6-5	225
Herman Stevenson	Duncan	T	6-3	235
Scott Smith	Hobart	T	6-4	255
Steve Lewis	OC Northeast	G	6-3	290
Richard Rose	Clinton	G	6-2	240
Ranny Meservy	Lawton	C	6-4	225
Mike Alexander	Duncan	SE	5-11	175
Melvin Gilliam	Tulsa Washington	QB	6-1	180
Glen Braxton	Idabel	FB	6-0	210
Mitchell Nash	Bartlesville	RB	5-9	180
Don Smitherman	McAlester	RB	5-11	180
Jeff Long	Watonga	P	5-11	160
Todd Thomsen	Sapulpa	K	6-2	180

Defense

Name	School	Pos.	Ht.	Wt.
Greg Williams	Durant	E	6-3	240
David Frolich	Del City	E	6-3	230
Eric Haley	Mustang	T	6-1	215
Kevin Luper	Adair	T	6-4	230
Jon Ed Brown	Norman	NG	6-0	205
Jeff Santee	Tulsa Kelley	LB	6-2	205
Woody Wilson	Shawnee	LB	6-0	190
Ronnie Biddle	Talihina	S	6-0	155
Alan Marcum	Pauls Valley	S	5-9	158
Darin Cosby	Ada	CB	6-1	179
Scott Myers	Chandler	CB	5-10	160

OKLAHOMA ALL-STATE FOOTBALL TEAM: 1984

SECOND TEAM

Offense

Name	School	Pos.	Ht.	Wt.
Bill Jones	Jay	TE	6-4	235
Joe Thompson	Ponca City	T	6-3	250
Mike Wise	Bartlesville	T	6-6	245
Steve Gibbs	Bristow	G	5-10	190
Wes Morris	Wilburton	G	6-3	225
Eddie Grant	Norman	C	6-3	235
Randy Summers	OC Grant	SE	6-0	165
Greg Neece	Edmond	QB	5-10	175
Mark Rice	Mustang	FB	6-1	210
Shell Henry	Picher	RB	6-0	185
David Cohimia	OC Heritage Hall	RB	6-0	195
Dusty Cozad	Sulphur	P	5-11	175
Jim Gottardi	Bartlesville	K	5-11	175

Defense

Name	School	Pos.	Ht.	Wt.
Leonard Lister	Clinton	E	5-11	185
Anthony Fisher	Atoka	E	6-1	205
Rick Hensley	Alva	T	6-2	215
Tracy Kuhlman	Chickasha	T	6-2	240
Jesse Wall	Midwest City	NG	5-11	235
Joe Jones	Sallisaw	LB	5-11	210
Tim Bates	Sulphur	LB	6-0	208
Adar Perkins	Tulsa East Central	S	6-1	180
Steve Kiefer	Kellyville	S	6-2	180
Derek Converse	Miami	GB	6-1	185
Chris Risenhoover	Tahlequah	CB	5-11	170

OKLAHOMA ALL-STATE FOOTBALL TEAM: 1985

FIRST TEAM

Offense

Name	School	Pos.	Ht.	Wt.
Trey Waller	Clinton	TE	6-1	215
Mike Martin	Morris	T	6-4	260
Roger Gibbs	Bixby	T	6-4	225
Bronco Hardgrave	Morris	G	6-3	245
Rod Slattery	Sallisaw	G	6-1	250
Bob Smith	Davis	C	6-2	230
Joey Witcher	Midwest City	SE	5-11	165
Mike Gundy	Midwest City	QB	6-0	180
Junior Thornburg	Wilburton	FB	6-0	205
Eldwin Raphel	Lawton Eisenhower	RB	6-0	170
Vernon Brown	Del City	RB	6-0	200
Matt Atyia	Seminole	K	5-10	165

Defense

Name	School	Pos.	Ht.	Wt.
Mike Hood	Sulphur	E	6-0	218
Scott Evans	Edmond	E	6-4	227
Mike Brown	Putnam City	T	6-3	253
Harold Jones	Bristow	T	6-4	275
Sim Drain III	Stillwater	LB	6-2	205
John Williamson	Moore	LB	5-10	180
Dirk Dean	Broken Bow	LB	6-2	190
Quinn Grovey	Duncan	DB	5-11	170
David Frost	Edmond	DB	6-2	180
Charles Thompson	Lawton	DB	5-10	165
Scott Barber	Pawnee	DB	5-11	175
Jim Marks	Sulphur	P	5-10	180

OKLAHOMA ALL-STATE FOOTBALL TEAM: 1985

SECOND TEAM

Offense

Name	School	Pos.	Ht.	Wt.
Steve Bartley	Enid	TE	5-11	180
Mike Sawatzky	Weatherford	T	6-3	248
Brad King	Putnam West	T	6-3	235
Buddy Holder	Durant	G	6-2	230
Butch Harris	Broken Bow	G	5-9	235
Jeff Duncan	Jay	C	6-0	210
Jerry Ashcraft	Hennessey	SE	5-9	160
Chris Smith	Ponca City	QB	6-2	180
Doug Watson	Del City	FB	6-0	205
Ricky Breath	Fox	RB	6-1	185
Rodney Jackson	Pauls Valley	RB	5-11	180
Kevin Strahorn	Blackwell	K	6-2	170

Defense

Name	School	Pos.	Ht.	Wt.
Raymond Roso	Tulsa Kelley	E	6-1	190
Kevin Cummins	Lindsay	E	6-3	200
Derrick Alexander	Tulsa Washington	T	6-3	235
Terron Manning	Muskogee	T	6-2	285
Allen Jordan	Sand Springs	LB	5-11	205
Tom Rivera	Purcell	LB	5-10	185
Bernard Rhone	OC Millwood	LB	5-10	180
Tim Neece	Sperry	DB	5-10	160
Craig Pruitt	Hobart	DB	5-10	160
Paul Behrman	Norman	DB	6-0	180
Mike Woodberry	MWC Carl Albert	DB	6-0	180
Vern Moore	OC Northeast	P	6-0	175

OKLAHOMA ALL-STATE FOOTBALL TEAM: 1986

FIRST TEAM

Offense

Name	School	Pos.	Ht.	Wt.	Coach
Ben Morrison	Tulsa McLain	QB	6-3	200	Melvin Driver
Glen Bell	Muskogee	RB	5-8	175	Ron Freeman
Mike Gaddis	MWC Carl Albert	RB	6-2	200	Al Miller
Rod Fisher	Lawton MacArthur	RB	6-1	185	Ron Hartline
John Whitworth	Owasso	C	6-3	225	Ray Hall
Josh Arrott	Edmond	T	6-4	230	Rick Jones
Marcus Wharry	Idabel	T	6-4	230	Fred Willis
Wes McCalip	Moore	G	6-3	245	D. Snokhous
Dalton Young	Sayre	G	6-1	280	D. Atterberry
Fallon Wacasey	Kansas	TE	6-8	230	Jon Hanna
Mitch Simons	Midwest City	WR	5-9	155	Dick Evans
Jamal West	Tulsa Washington	WR	6-2	190	Larry McGee
Sean Patterson	Putnam North	K	5-11	160	Ron Taylor

Defense

Name	School	Pos.	Ht.	Wt.	Coach
John Gaskill	Enid	E	6-1	195	Ron Lancaster
Brandon Colbert	El Reno	E	6-3	245	Tom Cobble
Randy Wallace	Midwest City	T	6-4	235	Dick Evans
Leslie Franklin	Enid	T	5-10	225	Ron Lancaster
Bobby Raynor	Idabel	LB	6-0	210	Fred Willis
Dan McAdams	Atoka	LB	6-2	200	Mike Lee
Marty Hatcher	Tulsa Memorial	LB	6-2	215	Mike Lloyd
Pinky Hurley	Fox	DB	5-10	175	Milton Cooper
Chris Melson	Ada	DB	6-0	180	L. McBroom
Brent Goins	Owasso	DB	6-4	180	Ray Hall
Norman Terry	Altus	DB	6-1	195	Darvis Cole
Sonny Feexico	Norman	P	6-3	220	C. L. Wade

OKLAHOMA ALL-STATE FOOTBALL TEAM: 1986

SECOND TEAM

Offense

Name	School	Pos.	Ht.	Wt.
Jackie Stafford	Moore	QB	5-10	160
Tony Brooks	Tulsa Washington	RB	6-2	195
Louis Curtis	Del City	RB	5-10	175
Darrell Wiggins	Kansas	RB	6-2	190
Mike Livingston	Clinton	C	6-2	220
Myron Hurst	Bristow	T	6-4	240
Jimmy Jestes	Pawnee	T	6-4	285
Todd McGuire	MWC Carl Albert	G	6-3	230
Mike Davidson	Hugo	G	6-3	250
Jim Carroll	Jay	WR	6-3	170
Barry Crosswhite	Hennessey	WR	5-9	160
Craig Hughes	Bixby	K	6-0	185

Defense

Name	School	Pos.	Ht.	Wt.
Brandt Lane	Tulsa Union	E	6-2	220
Jason Jouret	Ponca City	E	5-9	195
Leon Scarlett	Clinton	T	5-10	180
Horace Thompson	Tulsa Washington	T	6-3	240
Ben Ludwig	Putnam West	LB	6-1	215
Tony Tabor	Perkins	LB	5-9	190
Mike Bennett	Crescent	LB	6-0	245
Ivor Samilton	Tulsa Washington	DB	6-0	185
Greg DeQuasie	Midwest City	DB	5-11	180
Lance Swanson	Guymon	DB	6-1	180
Charles Thompson	Muskogee	DB	5-10	185
Sohn Seifried	Weatherford	P	5-10	160

OKLAHOMA ALL-STATE FOOTBALL TEAM: 1987

FIRST TEAM

Offense

Name	School	Pos.	Ht.	Wt.
Steve Dean	Ada	QB	6-2	180
Dewell Brewer	Lawton	RB	5-8	175
Tracy Scroggins	Cheoctah	RB	6-3	205
Charles Franks	OC John Marshall	WR	6-0	180
Shawn Davis	Tulsa McLain	WR	6-1	170
Amos Randall	Lawton MacArthur	OL	6-0	220
Stacey Satterwhite	Welch	OL	6-5	250
Lucian Twins	Clinton	OL	6-4	270
Jay Gilliam	Ardmore	OL	6-6	240
Gary Dees	Lawton	C	6-3	205
Lee Keith	McAlester	TE	6-4	200
Todd Wright	Stillwater	K	5-10	160

Defense

Name	School	Pos.	Ht.	Wt.
Jeff Frost	Putnam West	T	6-3	240
Mike Filson	Edmond	T	6-6	260
Aaron Tallman	Woodward	E	6-4	235
Toby Tillman	Owasso	E	6-2	255
Meech Shaw	Ponca City	LB	6-3	215
Shawn Jacoway	Sand Springs	LB	6-4	225
Bill Walter	OC Millwood	LB	6-2	205
Tink Collins	Ponca City	DB	5-10	175
Sean Wilson	Norman	DB	5-10	170
Marcus Shipp	OC Douglass	DB	6-3	180
Tony Levy	Wynnewood	DB	6-0	175
Larry Talbott	Kingfisher	P	6-4	225

OKLAHOMA ALL-STATE FOOTBALL TEAM: 1987

SECOND TEAM

Offense

Name	School	Pos.	Ht.	Wt.
Scott Epps	Jenks	QB	5-10	160
Charles Lister	Clinton	RB	6-0	205
Craig Garrison	Guymon	RB	5-11	185
Steve Magness	OC Heritage Hall	RB	6-1	175
Brett Thomas	Inola	WR	5-10	140
Randy Story	Altus	OL	6-1	250
John Drake	Mustang	OL	6-5	270
Vic Stachmus	McAlester	OL	6-4	270
John Fritch	OC McGuinness	OL	6-4	245
Bill Lovell	Muldrow	OL	6-4	280
Bryan Weems	Putnam West	TE	6-5	200
Jace Seals	Sand Springs	K	5-9	160

Defense

Name	School	Pos.	Ht.	Wt.
David Brooks	Tulsa Washington	DL	6-3	235
Ki Kiger	Tulsa Union	DL	6-3	235
Trevor Williams	Edmond	DL	6-3	240
Justin Hair	Tulsa Memorial	LB	6-1	210
Jay Don Johnson	Norman	LB	6-2	215
Rashid Lowe	Tulsa McLain	LB	6-1	200
Steve Dowdy	Bristow	LB	6-2	200
Jay Fleschman	Sand Springs	DB	6-1	190
Todd Alpers	Marlow	DB	6-3	175
Melvin Carter	OC John Marshall	DB	6-0	170
Shannon Colbert	El Reno	DB	6-3	180
Jimmy Byerly	Noble	P	6-3	185

OKLAHOMA ALL-STATE FOOTBALL TEAM: 1988

FIRST TEAM

Offense

Name	School	Pos.	Ht.	Wt.
Cale Gundy	Midwest City	QB	6-2	185
Dewell Brewer	Lawton	RB	5-8	195
Lamel Foreman	Del City	RB	6-0	185
Tyler Jack	Ada	RB	6-0	205
Mark Miller	Bartlesville	WR	6-0	170
Jason Louiver	Broken Bow	OL	6-5	280
Bobby Joe Hill	Marietta	OL	6-1	260
Robbie Fletcher	Maud	OL	6-5	260
Bret Hankins	Norman	OL	6-5	265
Ryan Patterson	Jenks	OL	6-3	240
Joey Mickey	OC Millwood	TE	6-7	250
Darin Booth	Guymon	K	5-9	175

Defense

Name	School	Pos.	Ht.	Wt.
Will Shields	Lawton	DL	6-4	270
Kevin Crutchmer	Lawton Eisenhower	DL	5-8	205
Chris Lovin	Anadarko	DL	5-11	215
Michael Coats	OC John Marshall	LB	6-2	220
Chris Bratcher	Edmond	LB	6-2	225
Tracy Price	McAlester	LB	6-0	215
Greg Prosak	Putnam North	LB	6-2	220
James Trapp	Lawton	DB	6-1	170
Aaron Goins	Owasso	DB	6-2	190
Charles Verner	Stillwater	DB	6-2	180
Shannon Colbert	El Reno	DB	6-1	165
Butch Huskey	Lawton Eisenhower	P	6-4	235

OKLAHOMA ALL-STATE FOOTBALL TEAM: 1988

SECOND TEAM

Offense

Name	School	Pos.	Ht.	Wt.
Travis Briggs	Tulsa Memorial	QB	6-2	205
Doug Neese	Edmond	RB	5-10	185
Eric Young	Broken Bow	RB	5-10	180
Maurice Sanders	Midwest City	WR	5-10	185
Ronn Hull	Spiro	TE	6-5	220
Gus Bradshaw	Claremore	OL	6-5	255
Donald Smith	OC Star Spencer	OL	6-4	245
Joe Bob Warner	Lawton	OL	6-3	240
Lance Harjo	Maud	OL	6-5	230
Mark Farquhar	T. Metro Christian	OL	6-1	220
Brett Thomas	Inola	WR	5-11	155
Artie Smith	Stillwater	TE	6-5	245
Brady Brus	Mustang	K	6-0	170

Defense

Name	School	Pos.	Ht.	Wt.
Russell Allen	OC Millwood	DL	6-7	245
Mike Butler	Muskogee	DL	6-3	255
Danny Ledbetter	Norman	DL	6-3	230
Nathan Goodyear	Enid	DL	6-2	230
Brad Vincent	Putnam West	LB	6-1	225
John Vasquez	Welch	LB	6-3	210
Otis Colbert	Tulsa Washington	LB	6-1	220
Chris McCarthey	Tuttle	LB	5-11	185
Brandon Brown	Ponca City	DB	5-10	170
Stephen Ford	Pauls Valley	DB	5-9	170
Richie Gandy	Ringling	DB	5-10	170
John Kerr	Morrison	DB	5-11	175
Bryan Jarrad	Webbers Falls	P	6-1	180

OKLAHOMA ALL-STATE FOOTBALL TEAM: 1989

FIRST TEAM

Offense

Name	School	Pos.	Ht.	Wt.
Cale Gundy	Midwest City	QB	6-1	190
Eric Young	Broken Arrow	RB	5-9	160
Brian Hamilton	Idabel	RB	6-0	200
Brad Norman	Ponca City West	RB	5-9	185
Darren Hasz	Jenks	WR	6-2	200
Kerry Sharpe	Checotah	OL	6-6	260
Heath Woods	Midwest City	OL	6-3	220
Chad Brown	Hennessey	OL	6-5	240
Scott Baker	Muskogee	OL	6-1	220
Cody Thompson	Mustang	OL	6-3	250
Rickey Brady	Ponca City West	TE	6-5	225
Rick Meyers	Broken Arrow	K	5-11	180

Defense

Name	School	Pos.	Ht.	Wt.
Max Whipple	Guymon	NG	6-0	240
Jason Gildon	Altus	GT	6-5	210
John Nemecek	Stillwater	DE	6-2	195
Tyler Williams	Edmond	DE	6-3	210
Mike Fields	Enid	LB	6-3	215
Raythan Smith	Tulsa Washington	LB	6-3	210
Tony Tubbs	Durant	LB	6-2	225
Drew Christmon	Midwest City	DB	5-11	200
Scott Harmon	Hominy	DB	5-10	176
Demond Sampson	Tulsa Washington	DB	6-0	180
Russell Jones	Mustang	DB	5-11	180
Jason Allen	Edmond	P	6-1	185

OKLAHOMA ALL-STATE FOOTBALL TEAM: 1989

SECOND TEAM

Offense

Name	School	Pos.	Ht.	Wt.
Dacona Smith	Wynnewood	QB	5-10	168
Russell Berrien	MWC Carl Albert	RB	5-11	180
Linn Marshall	Sulphur	RB	5-11	206
Gary Brown	Tulsa Memorial	WR	5-8	155
Jason Smith	Tulsa Edison	WR	6-1	180
Tim Martin	Weatherford	TE	6-4	218
Jeremy Stout	Edmond	OL	6-2	235
Leon Skillins	Tulsa Washington	OL	6-2	260
John Butler	Idabel	OL	6-2	265
Jim Creason	Elk City	OL	6-7	260
John O'Neil	Tulsa Edison	OL	6-6	250
Tate Wright	Stillwater	K	5-10	169

Defense

Name	School	Pos.	Ht.	Wt.
Steve Trotter	Guymon	DL	6-4	265
James Tiger	Mustang	DL	6-1	225
Shane Wallace	MWC Carl Albert	DL	6-1	248
Al Brown	Enid	DE	6-1	200
Derek Blackburn	Broken Arrow	DE	6-2	225
Kevin Britt	Okemah	LB	6-1	215
Jason Percy	Tulsa Holland Hall	LB	6-2	220
Joe Dale Stewart	Ringling	LB	6-2	174
Alex Goodpasture	Cheisea	DB	6-4	185
Todd Benway	Watonga	DB	6-0	188
Levi Moore	Tulsa Washington	DB	6-2	200
Richard Cantrell	Weleetka	P	6-4	180

OKLAHOMA ALL-STATE FOOTBALL TEAM: 1990

FIRST TEAM

Offense

Name	School	Pos.	Ht.	Wt.	Class
Shawn Snyder	Seminole	QB	6-1	185	Senior
Rafeal Denson	Ardmore	WR	5-8	165	Senior
Che Foster	Edmond	RB	6-3	237	Senior
Dustin Caldwell	Putnam North	RB	6-2	195	Senior
Dwight McFadden	Lawton Eisenhower	RB	6-0	180	Senior
JaJuan Penny	Tulsa Washington	WR	6-0	185	Senior
Reagan Allen	Enid	OL	6-5	265	Senior
Damon Taylor	Broken Arrow	OL	6-6	245	Senior
Tony Nagy	Tulsa Union	OL	6-5	250	Senior
Stuart Gage	Sand Springs	OL	6-5	285	Senior
Phillip Kinney	Lawton Eisenhower	OL	6-3	270	Senior

Defense

Name	School	Pos.	Ht.	Wt.	Class
David Campbell	OC Millwood	NG	6-2	270	Senior
Allen Gonzales	Jenks	DT	6-4	270	Senior
Pat Baker	Owasso	DT	6-4	280	Senior
Brent DeQuasie	Midwest City	DE	6-2	205	Senior
Syii Tucker	OC Douglass	DE	6-5	210	Senior
Drew Williams	Stillwater	LB	6-0	195	Senior
Jason Bufford	Crescent	LB	6-0	220	Senior
Chris Burk	Lawton MacArthur	LB	5-11	210	Senior
Chris Pollard	Lawton Eisenhower	DB	5-11	155	Senior
Kerry Rogers	Owasso	DB	6-2	180	Senior
Mark Mendoza	Tulsa Cascia Hall	DB	5-11	161	Senior

Specialists

Name	School	Pos.	Ht.	Wt.	Class
Jeremy Kennedy	OC Westmoore	K-TE	6-5	226	Senior
Scott Blanton	Norman	P	6-1	210	Senior
Mandrell Dean	OC Millwood	KR	6-0	170	Soph.

OKLAHOMA ALL-STATE FOOTBALL TEAM: 1990

SECOND TEAM

Offense

Name	School	Pos.	Ht.	Wt.	Class
Chris Cayot	Okeene	QB	5-9	190	Senior
Ben Bolen	Oologah	RB	6-1	185	Senior
Chad Byassee	Glenpool	WR	5-11	160	Senior
Terry Hawk	Putnam West	WR	6-0	175	Senior
Michael McDaniels	OC John Marshall	WR	6-2	190	Senior
Jeremy Gilstrap	Putnam North	TE	6-4	220	Senior
Jeff Dutton	Guthrie	OL	6-2	255	Senior
Brian Roberts	Norman	OL	6-3	255	Senior
Matt Maupin	Enid	OL	6-2	225	Senior
Norman Williams	Lawton Eisenhower	OL	5-11	220	Senior
Roger Pinson	Bristow	OL	6-3	225	Senior

Defense

Name	School	Pos.	Ht.	Wt.	Class
Matt Parker	Lawton Eisenhower	DL	6-3	240	Senior
Kenneth Burks	Enid	DL	6-2	300	Junior
Elgin Johnson	Tulsa McLain	DL	6-3	220	Senior
Bryan Hope	Oologah	LB	6-5	220	Senior
Thomas Chappelle	Tulsa Washington	LB	6-2	220	Senior
Scott Salmon	Tulsa Union	LB	6-0	215	Senior
Paul Cadell	Davis	LB	6-3	202	Senior
James Knott	Locust Grove	DB	6-2	175	Senior
Toby Parent	Warner	DB	5-11	180	Senior
Chad Redding	Minco	DB	5-11	170	Senior
Garrick McGee	Tulsa Washington	DB	6-3	180	Senior

Specialists

Name	School	Pos.	Ht.	Wt.	Class
Jeremy Woods	Midwest City	K-QB	6-3	195	Senior
Bill Wilson	Sallisaw	P	6-4	220	Senior
Mack Chambers	Spiro	KR	5-10	155	Senior

OKLAHOMA ALL-STATE FOOTBALL TEAM: 1991

FIRST TEAM

Offense

Name	School	Pos.	Ht.	Wt.	Class
Brad Woodard	Dewey	QB	6-2	190	Senior
James Allen	Wynnewood	RB	6-1	198	Junior
Jeff Frazier	OC Westmoore	RB	6-2	210	Senior
Greg Dean	Ada	RB	6-2	213	Senior
Mike McDaniels	OC John Marshall	WR	6-2	210	Senior
P. J. Mills	Enid	WR	6-1	185	Senior
Sean Wells	Jenks	OL	6-5	250	Senior
Joe Streich	Putnam North	OL	6-3	240	Senior
Chad Stanton	Ringling	OL	6-4	260	Senior
J. R. Conrad	Fairland	OL	6-5	275	Senior
Brant Robertson	Weatherford	OL	6-2	240	Senior

Defense

Name	School	Pos.	Ht.	Wt.	Class
Kenneth Burks	Enid	DL	6-1	315	Senior
Chris McCormick	Duncan	DL	5-11	235	Senior
Paul Miller	Edmond	DL	6-1	240	Senior
Jason Hall	Tulsa Union	DL	6-4	255	Senior
Demetrius Crowder	Eufaula	LB	6-3	230	Senior
Teddy McDade	Norman	LB	6-2	200	Senior
Willie Harrell	Enid	DE	6-0	215	Senior
Larry Bush	Ada	DB	6-1	193	Senior
Trent Fisher	Putnam North	DB	5-11	175	Senior
David Kerr	Morrison	DB	6-0	175	Senior
Adrian Paulden	Del City	DB	6-3	190	Senior

Specialists

Name	School	Pos.	Ht.	Wt.	Class
Lawson Vaughn	Edmond	K	6-1	161	Senior
Tim Daughtry	Midwest City	P	6-3	205	Junior
Dusty Hansen	Shattuck	KR	5-11	175	Senior

OKLAHOMA ALL-STATE FOOTBALL TEAM: 1991

SECOND TEAM

Offense

Name	School	Pos.	Ht.	Wt.	Class
Ben Rutz	Putnam West	QB	6-0	180	Senior
Willis Brown	Edmond	RB	5-9	165	Senior
Woody Hankins	Owasso	RB	5-9	185	Senior
Mike Minter	Lawton	RB	5-10	175	Senior
Jason Bennett	T. Metro Christian	WR	6-4	190	Senior
David Davison	Waurika	TE	6-2	200	Senior
Steve Malone	Ada	OL	6-1	270	Senior
Wade Harelson	Okemah	OL	6-4	223	Senior
Brian Newnam	Stroud	OL	6-4	225	Senior
Tom Procter	Broken Arrow	OL	6-3	235	Senior
Chris McKenzie	Moore	OL	6-3	274	Senior

Defense

Name	School	Pos.	Ht.	Wt.	Class
Jon Denton	Midwest City	DL	6-3	240	Senior
Travis Hildebrand	Mustang	DL	6-3	250	Senior
Dacquari Wilson	Tulsa Washington	DL	6-3	220	Senior
Stuart Osborn	Seminole	LB	6-2	205	Senior
Tyrell Peters	Norman	LB	6-1	200	Senior
Brian Turgeau	Broken Arrow	LB	6-2	215	Senior
Mike Odom	Poteau	LB	6-2	240	Senior
Brian Newberry	OC Westmoore	DB	6-3	193	Senior
Brandon Willis	Shawnee	DB	5-10	160	Senior
Phil Perkins	Jenks	DB	5-10	165	Senior
Waylon Jones	Okmulgee	DB	6-0	170	Senior

Specialists

Name	School	Pos.	Ht.	Wt.	Class
Joel Nicholson	OC McGuinness	K-WR	6-3	185	Senior
James Keesee	Lexington	P	6-3	180	Senior
Wes Galloway	Clinton	KR	5-10	175	Senior

OKLAHOMA ALL-STATE FOOTBALL TEAM: 1992

FIRST TEAM

Offense

Name	School	Pos.	Ht.	Wt.	Class
Tone Jones	Tulsa Washington	QB	6-0	175	Senior
James Allen	Wynnewood	RB	6-1	205	Senior
David Thompson	Okmulgee	RB	5-10	180	Senior
Mandrell Dean	OC Millwood	WR	6-0	185	Senior
Taj Johnson	Ardmore	WR	6-3	185	Senior
Alonzo Mayes	OC Douglass	TE	6-4	220	Senior
Barry Giles	Healdton	OL	6-7	255	Senior
John Lang	Marlow	OL	6-5	250	Senior
Brian Andrews	Edmond	OL	6-3	245	Senior
Robert Ingram	Ada	OL	6-5	275	Senior
Martin Chase	Lawton Eisenhower	OL	6-4	282	Junior

Defense

Name	School	Pos.	Ht.	Wt.	Class
Josh Heskew	Mustang	NG	6-3	242	Senior
Dusty Loveless	Norman	DT	6-3	285	Junior
Anthony Randle	Weatherford	DT	6-1	220	Senior
Tyrell Peters	Norman	LB	6-1	205	Senior
Carlton Hall	Midwest City	LB	6-2	230	Senior
Collin Rosenberg	Yukon	LB	6-4	225	Senior
Dion Wiggins	Ardmore	LB	5-11	220	Senior
Kris Lofton	OC Douglass	CB	6-2	190	Senior
Tracy Evans	Bixby	CB	5-11	178	Senior
Raymond Austin	Lawton Eisenhower	SS	5-11	172	Senior
Cal Hankins	Weatherford	FS	5-11	170	Senior

Specialist

Name	School	Pos.	Ht.	Wt.	Class
James Anderson	OC Westmoore	K	5-10	165	Senior
Brian Self	Norman	P	5-11	174	Senior
Chevin Hampton	Watonga	KR	5-9	150	Senior

OKLAHOMA ALL-STATE FOOTBALL TEAM: 1992

SECOND TEAM

Offense

Name	School	Pos.	Ht.	Wt.	Class
Cornelius Davis	OC Millwood	QB	6-1	200	Senior
Justin Paul	Ringling	RB	5-10	165	Senior
Chris Jones	Jenks	RB	6-0	170	Junior
Anthony Eubanks	Spiro	WR	6-3	175	Senior
Marcus Nash	Edmond	WR	6-3	180	Junior
Brad Westmoreland	Haskell	TE	6-6	205	Senior
Brad Smith	OC Westmoore	OL	6-4	260	Senior
Diron Robinson	Midwest City	OL	6-3	235	Senior
Jeremiah Johnson	Bixby	OL	6-2	270	Senior
Stanley Thomas	Ringling	OL	6-3	270	Senior
Chad Dotson	Wynnewood	OL	6-0	195	Senior

Defense

Name	School	Pos.	Ht.	Wt.	Class
Philip Wilson	Newcastle	DL	6-1	220	Senior
Creighton Solomon	El Reno	DL	6-2	295	Senior
Willie Hill	Broken Bow	DL	6-3	225	Senior
Rod Humphrey	Tulsa Washington	LB	6-1	210	Senior
J. J. Eckert	Tahiequah	LB	6-0	190	Senior
Stephen Alexander	Chickasha	DE	6-5	215	Junior
Jay Patterson	Jenks	DE	6-4	195	Senior
Mike Owens	Norman	DB	6-1	175	Senior
Len Sexton	MWC Carl Albert	DB	5-11	180	Senior
Richard Norman	Plainview	DB	6-1	192	Senior
Tim Shadlow	Hominy	DB	6-2	165	Senior

Specialists

Name	School	Pos.	Ht.	Wt.	Class
Brock Zimmerman	Del City	K	6-1	200	Senior
Tim Daughtry	Midwest City	P	6-3	215	Senior
Jason Jacoby	Yukon	KR	5-10	165	Senior

OKLAHOMA ALL-STATE FOOTBALL TEAM: 1993

FIRST TEAM

Offense

Name	School	Pos.	Ht.	Wt.	Class
Craig Strickland	MWC Carl Albert	QB	6-2	190	Senior
Bennie Butler	Del City	RB	6-1	190	Junior
Chris Jones	Jenks	RB	5-10	175	Senior
Marcus Nash	Edmond	WR	6-4	190	Senior
Todd Perry	Seminole	WR	5-10	170	Senior
Stephen Alexander	Chickasha	TE	6-6	225	Senior
Russell Brown	Bristow	OL	6-2	260	Senior
Greg Moyer	Stillwater	OL	6-4	240	Senior
Russell Gaskamp	Weatherford	OL	6-5	272	Senior
Jeremy Shadrick	Tulsa Union	OL	6-4	275	Senior
Kelly Gregg	Edmond	OL	6-2	235	Junior

Defense

Name	School	Pos.	Ht.	Wt.	Class
Diron Robinson	Midwest City	DL	6-3	250	Senior
Mitch Minick	Bixby	DL	6-2	270	Senior
Dusty Loveless	Norman	DL	6-2	301	Senior
Martin Chase	Lawton Eisenhower	DL	6-2	280	Senior
Jonathan Brown	Tulsa Washington	DL	6-6	250	Senior
Travis Hartfield	Watonga	LB	6-2	195	Senior
Jason Wiggins	Newcastle	LB	6-1	215	Senior
Richard Robinson	Lawton	LB	5-11	215	Senior
John Fitzgerald	Seminole	DB	6-4	190	Senior
Paul Phipps	Jenks	DB	5-11	195	Senior
Reggie Gaskins	Cushing	DB	5-10	175	Senior

Specialists

Name	School	Pos.	Ht.	Wt.	Class
Jeremy Alexander	Claremore	K	5-11	170	Senior
Rusty Rushing	Owasso	P-DB	6-1	170	Junior
Mario Bryson	Clinton	KR	5-10	165	Senior

OKLAHOMA ALL-STATE FOOTBALL TEAM: 1993

SECOND TEAM

Offense

Name	School	Pos.	Ht.	Wt.	Class
Warren Foust	Midwest City	QB	6-3	205	Senior
Demond Parker	Tulsa Washington	RB	5-9	175	Junior
Chris Stewart	Chickasha	RB	5-9	180	Senior
Sean Love	OC John Marshall	WR	5-10	170	Junior
Mike Jones	Casady	WR	6-3	195	Senior
Matt McCormick	Duncan	TE	6-5	228	Senior
Tim Macias	Putnam City	OL	6-4	240	Senior
Shane Wyatt	Chickasha	OL	6-2	265	Senior
Mark Thomas	Collinsville	OL	6-3	270	Senior
Denis Junker	Jenks	OL	6-2	250	Senior
Wes Richardson	Watonga	OL	6-2	285	Senior

Defense

Name	School	Pos.	Ht.	Wt.	Class
Dale Allen	Wynnewood	DL	6-4	230	Senior
Brian Pinson	Bristow	DL	6-5	235	Senior
Tim Martin	Claremore Sequoyah	DL	6-4	225	Senior
Neil Whitworth	Frederick	DL	6-5	220	Senior
Travis Adams	Noble	LB	6-1	220	Senior
Lance West	Jenks	LB	5-10	175	Senior
Jeremy Gay	Ardmore	LB	6-1	215	Senior
Garrett Phynes	Ada	DB	6-0	178	Senior
Jered Guinn	Maud	DB	6-3	200	Senior
Robert McQuarters	Tulsa Washington	DB	5-11	170	Junior
Mike Carter	Lawton	DB	5-11	165	Junior

Specialist

Name	School	Pos.	Ht.	Wt.	Class
Chad Kositzky	OC Westmoore	K	6-1	170	Senior
Bremt Antwine	Weatherford	p	5-11	177	Senior
Shawn Dahl	Bamsdall	KR	5-10	165	Senior

OKLAHOMA ALL-STATE FOOTBALL TEAM: 1994

FIRST TEAM

Offense

Name	School	Pos.	Ht.	Wt.	Class
Justin Fuente	Tulsa Union	QB	6-3	210	Senior
Eric Bernard	Tulsa Union	RB	5-10	175	Senior
Bennie Butler	Del City	RB	6-1	192	Senior
Richie Calmus	Jenks	RB	6-1	175	Senior
Willie Grissom	OC John Marshall	WR	5-10	175	Senior
Jason Freeman	Muskogee	TE	6-3	230	Senior
Jody Crook	Velma-Alma	OL	6-3	258	Senior
Bryan Alley	Grove	OL	6-5	269	Senior
Ryan Farley	Owasso	OL	6-3	265	Senior
Ron James	Pawnee	OL	6-4	265	Senior
Jason Owen	Midwest City	OL	6-3	265	Senior

Defense

Name	School	Pos.	Ht.	Wt.	Class
Casey Bookout	Stroud	DL	6-5	260	Senior
Kelly Gregg	Edmond North	DL	6-2	255	Senior
Kevin Kemp	Wewoka	DL	6-6	296	Senior
Jerry Wisne	Jenks	DL	6-7	282	Senior
Joe Griffin	Putnam West	LB	5-9	200	Senior
Chad Mead	Woodward	LB	6-1	220	Senior
Kqorea Willlis	Watonga	LB	6-4	24	Senior
Mike Carter	Lawton	DB	5-9	160	Senior
Raymond Cato	Midwest City	DB	6-1	195	Senior
Brandon Daniels	Ada	DB	6-1	195	Senior
R.W. McQuarters	Tulsa Washington	DB	6-0	180	Senior

Specialists

Name	School	Pos.	Ht.	Wt.	Class
Tim Sydnes	Putnam West	K	6-1	180	Senior
Ryan Benn	Frederick	P	6-2	185	Senior
Reggie Skinner	White Oak	KR	5-8	205	Senior

OKLAHOMA ALL-STATE FOOTBALL TEAM: 1994

SECOND TEAM

Offense

Name	School	Pos.	Ht.	Wt.	Class
Brad Cornelsen	Texhoma	QB	5-11	160	Senior
Charlie Higgins	Hominy	RB	5-11	190	Senior
Barry Odom	Ada	RB	6-1	193	Senior
Damond Parker	Tulsa Washington	RB	5-11	175	Senior
Jason Blackwell	Mustang	WR	6-2	170	Senior
Dustin Steele	Tulsa Union	WR	5-10	185	Senior
Brent Baker	Muskogee	OL	6-3	230	Senior
Fred Goodwin	Norman	OL	6-4	270	Senior
Taber Deblanc	Edmond North	OL	6-2	235	Senior
Andy Potts	OC Westmoore	OL	6-7	260	Senior
Cameron Roy	Lawton	OL	6-4	285	Senior

Defense

Name	School	Pos.	Ht.	Wt.	Class
Aaron Findley	Wewoka	DL	6-6	285	Senior
Kevin Scroggins	Watonga	DL	6-2	275	Senior
Jeremy Wilson	Jones	DL	6-2	265	Senior
Wesley Woodward	Midwest City	DL	6-3	267	Senior
Mike Colston	OC Douglass	LB	5-11	205	Senior
Jared Dunivan	Morrison	LB	6-1	217	Senior
Jeremy McClure	Tahlequah	LB	6-3	215	Senior
Byron Cherry	Broken Bow	DB	6-2	190	Senior
Corey Ivy	Moore	DB	5-9	175	Senior
Ryan Logan	Enid	DB	5-10	195	Senior
Bruce Sutton	Ada	DB	6-2	173	Senior

Specialists

Name	School	Pos.	Ht.	Wt.	Class
Jon Hillman	Tecumseh	K	5-11	170	Senior
Mike Coyle	Sperry	P	5-9	160	Senior
Sean Love	OC John Marshall	KR	5-10	175	Senior

OKLAHOMA ALL-STATE FOOTBALL TEAM: 1995

FIRST TEAM

Offense

Name	School	Pos.	Ht.	Wt.	Class
Brandon Daniels	Ada	QB	6-1	207	Senior
Justin Matthews	OC John Marshall	RB	5-11	190	Senior
Sedric Jones	Altus	RB	6-4	239	Senior
Joe Thomas	Broken Bow	RB	6-4	210	Senior
Ananias Carson	Jenks	WR	5-10	175	Senior
Matt Anderson	Moore	TE	6-3	230	Senior
Scott Kempenich	Wagoner	OL	6-7	275	Senior
Steve Williams	Sapulpa	OL	6-4	260	Senior
Zac Akin	Putnam North	OL	6-4	240	Senior
John Williams	Putnam City	OL	6-4	264	Senior
Kenneth Riddle	Prague	OL	6-4	265	Senior

Defense

Name	School	Pos.	Ht.	Wt.	Class
Ryan Allen	Enid	DL	6-5	256	Senior
Dustin Taylor	Durant	DL	6-2	280	Senior
Jeremy Wilson	Jones	DL	6-2	272	Senior
Jake Crissup	Jenks	LB	5-11	195	Senior
Donavon Laviness	Midwest City	LB	6-0	200	Senior
Kevin Brown	McAlester	LB	6-2	235	Senior
Kenyattta Wright	Vian	LB	6-2	225	Senior
Vernon Maxwell	Midwest City	DB	6-3	205	Senior
Rodney Rideau	Midwest City	DB	5-11	185	Senior
Mike Woods	Del City	DB	5-11	170	Senior
Kevin Isham	Frederick	DB	6-3	215	Senior

Specialists

Name	School	Pos.	Ht.	Wt.	Class
Evan Luttrell	Midwest City	K	5-10	170	Senior
Eric Stevenson	Crescent	KR	6-4	240	Senior

OKLAHOMA ALL-STATE FOOTBALL TEAM: 1995

SECOND TEAM

Offense

Name	School	Pos.	Ht.	Wt.	Class
Brian Presley	Jenks	QB	6-0	175	Senior
Chris Claybon	Tulsa Union	RB	5-10	170	Senior
T. J. McMurray	Hobart	RB	5-11	170	Senior
Chris Johnson	Chickasha	RB	6-0	227	Senior
Julius McMillan	Altus	WR	6-0	185	Junior
Ryan Humphrey	Tulsa Washington	TE	6-7	200	Junior
Eric Bartlow	Midwest City	OL	6-3	265	Senior
Ryan Ambrose	Checotah	OL	6-4	275	Senior
Lee Sutter	OC John Marshall	OL	6-0	290	Senior
Jered Miller	Welch	OL	6-5	255	Senior
Terrance Anderson	Stillwater	OL	6-5	255	Senior

Defense

Name	School	Pos.	Ht.	Wt.	Class
Denisto Cook	Stillwater	DL	6-4	280	Senior
Robert Falling	Vinita	DL	6-3	290	Senior
Jerry Arnold	Broken Arrow	DL	6-2	210	Senior
Itis Atkinson	Lawton MacArthur	LB	5-11	185	Senior
Aaron Compton	Cleveland	LB	6-2	235	Senior
J. C. Thomas	Idabel	LB	6-1	240	Senior
Brad Harris	Sand Springs	LB	6-2	220	Senior
Johnnie Jones	Lawton Eisenhower	DB	5-8	155	Senior
Damian Everette	Lawton MacArthur	DB	5-10	185	Senior
Darin Kapella	Davis	DB	6-1	175	Senior
Gary Manuel	Snyder	DB	5-6	185	Senior

Specialists

Name	School	Pos.	Ht.	Wt.	Class
Jeremy Thompson	Clinton	K	5-10	173	Senior
Mike Wilson	Marlow Central	P	6-1	195	Senior
Corky Martin	Claremore Sequoyah	KR	5-11	215	Senior

OKLAHOMA ALL-STATE FOOTBALL TEAM: 1996

FIRST TEAM

Offense

Name	School	Pos.	Ht.	Wt.	Class
Jarrod Reese	Seminole	QB	6-3	205	Senior
Eric Gooden	Midwest City	RB	6-3	215	Senior
Terrance Gaines	Frederick	RB	5-10	220	Senior
Tony Newsome	OC John Marshall	WR	6-2	200	Senior
Ahmed Kabba	OC Westmoore	WR	6-4	191	Senior
Ryan Humphrey	Tulsa Washington	TE	6-7	215	Senior
Matt Howard	Yukon	OL	6-1	295	Senior
Lynn Larabee	OC Western Heights	OL	6-5	261	Senior
DeVane Robinson	Midwest City	OL	6-4	260	Senior
Jon Rutherford	Midwest City	OL	6-4	260	Senior
Steve Wiedower	Tulsa Union	OL	6-3	250	Senior

Defense

Name	School	Pos.	Ht.	Wt.	Class
Darryl Bright	Tulsa Washington	DL	6-5	240	Senior
Cory Callens	Jenks	DL	6-3	250	Senior
Bary Holleyman	Putnam North	DL	6-6	235	Senior
Jason Lohr	Jenks	DL	6-3	260	Junior
Tango McCauley	OC John Marshall	DL	6-5	250	Senior
James Enix	Moore	LB	6-1	210	Senior
Seth Littrell	Muskogee	LB	6-0	210	Senior
Bubba Babb	Ada	DB	6-3	200	Senior
J. T. Thatcher	Norman	DB	6-0	180	Senior
Paul Jones	Wewoka	DB	6-3	185	Senior
B. J. Tiger	Tulsa Washington	DB	6-2	195	Senior

Specialists

Name	School	Pos.	Ht.	Wt.	Class
Jeff Ferguson	Tulsa Holland Hall	K	5-11	160	Senior
Josh Fidler	Jenks	P	5-10	188	Senior
Julius McMillan	Altus	KR	5-11	171	Senior

OKLAHOMA ALL-STATE FOOTBALL TEAM: 1996

SECOND TEAM

Offense

Name	School	Pos.	Ht.	Wt.	Class
Matt Holliday	Stillwater	QB	6-4	212	Junior
Stanley Peters	Pauls Valley	RB	5-9	175	Senior
Brian Thomas	Ada	RB	6-2	220	Senior
Aaron Lockett	Tulsa Washington	WR	5-9	160	Senior
Marcus Jones	Stillwater	WR	5-9	175	Senior
Trent Smith	Clinton	TE	6-5	220	Junior
Chad Blackburn	Duncan	OL	6-3	260	Senior
Jake Harriger	Broken Arrow	OL	6-3	265	Senior
James Miller	McAlester	OL	6-4	300	Senior
Jon Oliver	Putnam North	OL	6-6	275	Senior
Andy Wisne	Jenks	OL	6-3	250	Senior

Defense

Name	School	Pos.	Ht.	Wt.	Class
Dujuan Bowie	Tulsa Rogers	DL	6-3	265	Senior
Andre Butler	Lawton Eisenhower	DL	6-3	240	Senior
Marcellous Rivers	OC Douglass	DL	6-4	225	Senior
Frank Romero	Moore	DL	6-5	230	Junior
Jason Harding	Tulsa Washington	LB	6-1	240	Senior
Jason Kilmer	Washington	LB	6-0	190	Junior
Dusty McSwane	Lawton MacArthur	LB	6-2	190	Senior
Tony Peters	Tulsa McLain	LB	6-3	265	Senior
Jason Benson	Duncan	DB	6-0	180	Senior
Roderick Burdine	Prague	DB	5-10	190	Senior
Jeromy Toles	Broken Arrow	DB	6-3	180	Senior

Specialists

Name	School	Pos.	Ht.	Wt.	Class
Ben Roberts	Tulsa Union	K	5-11	155	Senior
Roy York	Stroud	P	6-0	195	Senior
Jason Crawford	Clinton	KR	5-11	195	Senior

OKLAHOMA ALL-STATE FOOTBALL TEAM: 1997

FIRST TEAM

Offense

Name	School	Pos.	Ht.	Wt.	Class
Matt Holliday	Stillwater	QB	6-4	215	Senior
Jay Hunt	MWC Carl Albert	RB	5-11	190	Senior
Josh Scobey	Del City	RB	6-0	200	Senior
Rockwell Armstrong	MWC Carl Albert	WR	6-3	175	Senior
Lawson Giddings	McAlester	WR	6-2	180	Senior
Trent Smith	Clinton	TE	6-6	220	Senior
Kyle Bookout	Stroud	OL	6-7	295	Senior
Lute Croy	Duncan	OL	6-2	290	Senior
Sean Mahan	Jenks	OL	6-4	245	Senior
Jason Russell	Putnam City	OL	6-5	260	Senior
Mike Skinner	Tahlequah	OL	6-6	285	Senior

Defense

Name	School	Pos.	Ht.	Wt.	Class
Brad Hawkins	Jenks	DL	6-3	225	Senior
Shane Kennon	Putnam North	DL	6-4	240	Senior
Jason Lohr	Jenks	DL	6-2	275	Senior
Frank Romero	Moore	DL	6-5	240	Senior
Rocky Calmus	Jenks	LB	6-4	240	Senior
Pedro Negron	Sand Springs	LB	5-10	190	Junior
Tanner Reynolds	Chickasha	LB	6-3	220	Senior
Brandon Jones	Frederick	DB	6-3	205	Senior
Brian Madden	Lawton Eisenhower	DB	6-2	205	Senior
DeMarco McCleskey	Claremore	DB	6-1	200	Senior
Brian Steele	Spiro	DB	5-11	190	Senior

Specialist

Name	School	Pos.	Ht.	Wt.	Class
Josh Brown	Foyil	K	6-2	180	Senior
Jake Bolig	Moore	P	5-11	180	Senior
Jason Kilmer	Washington	KR	6-0	200	Senior

OKLAHOMA ALL-STATE FOOTBALL TEAM: 1997

SECOND TEAM

Offense

Name	School	Pos.	Ht.	Wt.	Class
Jason White	Tuttle	QB	6-2	200	Junior
Jason Broom	Sapulpa	RB	5-9	205	Senior
T. J. Leon	Norman	RB	6-0	200	Senior
Jared Mathias	Oologah	RB	6-2	210	Senior
Trey Waters	Stillwater	WR	6-2	185	Senior
Ronnie Roberts	McLoud	TE	6-7	250	Senior
Dustin Files	Newcastle	OL	6-2	260	Senior
John Sturch	Moore	OL	6-3	235	Senior
Russell Mock	Yukon	OL	6-0	225	Senior
Justin Mock	Yukon	OL	6-0	230	Senior
Seth Adams	Wyandotte	OL	6-5	200	Senior

Defense

Name	School	Pos.	Ht.	Wt.	Class
Justin Dixon	Jenks	DL	6-2	230	Senior
Mark Mallory	Sand Springs	DL	6-7	240	Senior
Jesse Fore	Claremore Sequoyah	DL	6-6	260	Senior
Travis Townsell	Berryhill	LB	5-11	195	Senior
Derrick Johnson	Duncan	LB	6-1	190	Senior
Joey Crawford	Bristow	LB	6-3	230	Senior
Jeremy Armstead	Tulsa Central	LB	6-3	205	Junior
Brett Butler	Jenks	DB	6-2	175	Senior
Chris Massey	Spiro	DB	6-0	190	Junior
Richard Schwarz	Yukon	DB	6-0	180	Junior
Carlos Salazar	Turpin	DB	5-7	150	Senior

Specialists

Name	School	Pos.	Ht.	Wt.	Class
Shane Goldsby	Moore	K	5-11	165	Senior
Nik McDaniel	Poteau	P	6-0	185	Senior
Milen Darby	Midwest City	KR	5-9	185	Senior

OKLAHOMA ALL-STATE FOOTBALL TEAM: 1998

FIRST TEAM

Offense

Name	School	Pos.	Ht.	Wt.	Class
Josh Blankenship	Tulsa Union	QB	6-3	205	Senior
C J. Hammons	Moore	RB	5-11	175	Senior
Danny Morris	Tulsa Union	RB	5-11	180	Senior
Richard Schwarz	Yukon	RB	6-0	185	Senior
Michael Johnson	Tulsa Union	WR	6-4	220	Senior
Josh Tucker	Moore	TE	6-5	235	Senior
Charlie Atteberry	Elk City	OL	6-4	228	Senior
Ian Hobbs	OC Westmoore	OL	6-4	245	Senior
Ross Lassley	Mustang	OL	6-5	246	Senior
Steve Pollard	Muskogee	OL	6-4	350	Senior
Mike Rose	MWC Carl Albert	OL	6-2	250	Senior

Defense

Name	School	Pos.	Ht.	Wt.	Class
Kory Klein	Tulsa Union	DL	6-3	265	Senior
Aaron McConnell	Midwest City	DL	6-3	260	Senior
Ty Sanders	Chickasha	DL	6-2	270	Senior
Josh Holman	Sallisaw	LB	6-1	180	Senior
Greg Richmond	OC Douglass	LB	6-2	225	Senior
Justin Thomas	OC Star Spencer	LB	6-3	235	Senior
Brandon Hurst	MWC Carl Albert	DB	5-10	192	Senior
Chris Massey	Spiro	DB	6-1	198	Senior
Matt McCoy	Jenks	DB	6-0	190	Senior
Jason White	Tuttle	DB	6-3	220	Senior
Rashaun Woods	OC Millwood	DB	6-3	180	Senior

Specialists

Name	School	Pos.	Ht.	Wt.	Class
Cort Moffitt	Tulsa Washington	K	6-4	210	Senior
Ben Bowling	Jenks	p	6-3	210	Senior
Bryan Blew	Edmond North	KR	5-11	185	Senior

OKLAHOMA ALL-STATE FOOTBALL TEAM: 1998

SECOND TEAM

Offense

Name	School	Pos.	Ht.	Wt.	Class
Aso Pogi	Lawton	QB	6-4	205	Senior
Adebayo Ayodele	Owasso	RB	5-4	171	Senior
Larry Dupree	Luther	RB	5-8	185	Senior
Josh Copeland	Oologah	WR	6-2	185	Senior
Anthony Johnson	Tulsa Washington	WR	6-3	180	Senior
Matt Baldischwiler	Newcastle	TE	6-3	230	Senior
Matt Black	Claremore	OL	6-3	275	Junior
John Hayhurst	Choctaw	OL	6-4	275	Senior
Marc Liggins	OC John Marshall	OL	6-7	325	Senior
Brandon Parker	Pocola	OL	6-5	350	Senior
Brent Polwart	Enid	OL	6-7	304	Senior

Defense

Name	School	Pos.	Ht.	Wt.	Class
Tim Burrough	OC Westmoore	DL	6-1	230	Senior
Thomas Hill	Tulsa Hale	DL	6-5	250	Senior
Dwayne Mcintosh	Tulsa Washington	DL	6-6	230	Senior
Jeff Harbert	Tishomingo	LB	5-10	193	Senior
Jarrod Roach	Watonga	LB	6-2	215	Senior
Pedro Negron	Sand Springs	LB	5-10	210	Senior
Casey Bowers	Fairland	DB	6-0	170	Senior
Elbert Craig	OC Millwood	DB	6-2	190	Senior
Brandon Green	Adair	DB	6-1	175	Junior
Donald Ponds	OC Northeast	DB	5-10	175	Senior
Michael Thompson	Bristow	DB	6-2	180	Senior

Specialists

Name	School	Pos.	Ht.	Wt.	Class
Bruce Kjellander	OC Westmoore	K	5-0	156	Senior
Graham Colton	OC Heritage Hall	P	6-0	175	Junior
Wes Welker	OC Heritage Hall	KR	5-9	176	Junior

OKLAHOMA ALL-STATE FOOTBALL TEAM: 1998

THIRD TEAM

Offense

Name	School	Pos.	Ht.	Wt.	Class
Andrew Linn	OC Grant	QB	6-2	180	Senior
Tarik Abdullah	Spiro	RB	5-10	190	Senior
Anthony Cato	Glenpool	RB	5-7	150	Senior
Romby Bryant	OC Western Heights	WR	6-1	170	Senior
Riley Riggs	Edmond Memorial	WR	6-2	180	Senior
Jeremy Shockey	Ada	WR	6-3	195	Senior
Kevin Dyer	Chickasha	OL	6-1	230	Senior
Jeremy Gray	Coweta	OL	6-4	260	Senior
Courtney Kamer	Altus	OL	6-4	275	Senior
Brian Martin	Mustang	OL	6-6	340	Senior
Dustin Price	Edmond Memorial	OL	6-3	285	Junior

Defense

Name	School	Pos.	Ht.	Wt.	Class
John Factor	Moore	DL	6-0	265	Senior
Harrison Frost	Edmond Santa Fe	DL	6-7	220	Senior
J. J. Ramsey	Tulsa Cascia Hall	DL	6-1	235	Senior
Sam Rayburn	Chickasha	DL	6-5	270	Senior
Jeremy Beard	Rush Springs	LB	5-9	185	Senior
Luke Coe	Deer Creek	LB	6-3	205	Senior
Mitchell Lawson	Lawton	LB	5-9	195	Senior
Tyler Williams	Cleveland	LB	6-3	228	Senior
Brad Bryan	Norman North	DB	6-3	195	Senior
Tyler Marsh	Elk City	DB	5-9	178	Senior
Landon Wood	Tishomingo	DB	5-9	140	Senior

Specialists

Name	School	Pos.	Ht.	Wt.	Class
Jason Thomason	Oologah	K	6-1	182	Junior
Steve Davis	Mounds	P	5-11	175	Senior
Josh Hightower	Davenport	KR	5-9	160	Junior

OKLAHOMA ALL-STATE FOOTBALL TEAM: 1999

FIRST TEAM

Offense

Name	School	Pos.	Ht.	Wt.	Class
James Kilian	Medford	QB	6-4	220	Senior
Mario Hain	Ardmore	RB	5-11	190	Senior
John James	Putnam North	RB	5-10	190	Senior
Brian Odom	Ada	RB	6-0	195	Senior
Antonio Perkins	Lawton	WR	6-0	170	Senior
Lance Donley	Weatherford	TE	6-4	225	Senior
Chris Akin	Weatherford	OL	6-3	280	Senior
Matt Black	Claremore	OL	6-2	288	Senior
Drew Horton	Jenks	OL	6-4	275	Senior
Zack Newby	Putnam North	OL	6-4	275	Senior
Cliff Takawana	Ardmore	OL	6-3	300	Senior

Defense

Name	School	Pos.	Ht.	Wt.	Class
Clay Coe	Deer Creek	DT	6-3	260	Senior
J. T. Norton	Chickasha	DT	6-3	315	Senior
Adam Doiron	Duncan	DE	6-4	265	Senior
L. J. Williams	Clinton	DE	5-11	210	Senior
Johnny Bizzell	MWC Carl Albert	LB	6-1	225	Senior
Ronbrose Jones	Bristow	LB	6-4	235	Senior
Teddy Lehman	Fort Gibson	LB	6-1	225	Senior
Darren Flowers	Moore	DB	5-9	165	Senior
Jerome Janet	Tulsa Union	DB	6-0	178	Junior
Bobby Klinck	Jenks	DB	5-10	190	Junior
Darrell Wimberly	Tulsa Union	DB	5-10	192	Senior

Specialists

Name	School	Pos.	Ht.	Wt.	Class
Jason Thomason	Oologah	K	6-1	210	Senior
Graham Colton	OC Heritage Hall	P	6-1	180	Senior
Wes Welker	OC Heritage Hall	KR	5-9	185	Senior

OKLAHOMA ALL-STATE FOOTBALL TEAM: 1999

SECOND TEAM

Offense

Name	School	Pos.	Ht.	Wt.	Class
Justin Southerland	Tahiquh	QB	6-3	210	Senior
Marshell Chiles	El Reno	RB	5-10	190	Junior
Seymore Shaw	Shawnee	RB	6-0	210	Junior
Eric Brown	Putnam City	WR	6-1	175	Senior
Ataleo Ford	Ardmore	WR	6-2	185	Senior
J. D. McCoy	Moore	TE	6-3	240	Senior
Jammal Brown	Lawton MacArthur	OL	6-6	310	Senior
DeMarcus Carroll	Okmulgee	OL	6-1	300	Senior
Nick Huffaker	Healdton	OL	6-7	321	Senior
Dustin Price	Edmond Memorial	OL	6-2	300	Senior
Derek Rogers	Tulsa Union	OL	6-3	240	Senior

Defense

Name	School	Pos.	Ht.	Wt.	Class
Ben Bule	Broken Arrow	DT	6-2	280	Senior
Kyle Coulter	Sapulpa	DE	6-2	230	Senior
Kyle Williams	Plainview	DE	6-5	255	Senior
Kendall Bryson	McAlester	LB	6-1	230	Senior
Dan Cody	Ada	LB	6-4	230	Senior
Gary Smith	Clinton	LB	6-1	190	Senior
Luke Turner	Jenks	LB	5-9	215	Senior
Buddy Blair	Jenks	DB	6-1	180	Senior
Brandon Green	Adair	DB	6-1	175	Senior
Jeremy Kliewer	Fairview	DB	5-10	185	Senior
Scott Klufa	Tonkawa	DB	5-9	175	Senior

Specialists

Name	School	Pos.	Ht.	Wt.	Class
Blake Ferguson	Bixby	K	6-1	175	Senior
Mickey Nichol	Broken Arrow	P	6-2	205	Senior
Chay Nease	Thomas	KR	6-1	192	Senior

OKLAHOMA ALL-STATE FOOTBALL TEAM: 1999

THIRD TEAM

Offense

Name	School	Pos.	Ht.	Wt.	Class
James Smith	Deer Creek	QB	6-2	190	Senior
Chris Johnson	Haskell	RB	6-0	185	Senior
Renaldo Works	Tulsa Washington	RB	6-1	205	Senior
Luke Dobbins	Tahlequah	WR	6-1	185	Senior
David Porter	Owasso	WR	6-1	195	Senior
Patrick Nally	Tulsa Bishop Kelley	TE	6-5	230	Senior
Ben Culp	Sand Springs	OL	6-5	300	Senior
Tim Jackson	Lawton Eisenhower	OL	6-6	270	Senior
Mike Little	El Reno	OL	5-10	235	Senior
Josh Reed	Sand Springs	OL	6-6	245	Senior
Kenny Gould	Altus	OL	6-3	261	Senior

Defense

Name	School	Pos.	Ht.	Wt.	Class
Kyle Holt	Clinton	DT	6-2	240	Senior
Fath Carter	El Reno	DE	6-4	215	Senior
Josh Hamblin	MWC Carl Albert	DE	6-3	205	Senior
Brian Donahue	Tulsa Cascia Hall	LB	6-1	195	Senior
Kevin Kemp	Pawhuska	LB	6-1	195	Senior
Tracy McGuire	Spiro	LB	6-2	235	Senior
Austin Auringer	OC Westmoore	DB	5-10	175	Senior
Drew Beard	Rush Springs	DB	5-10	165	Senior
Matt Pollard	Poteau	DB	6-2	195	Senior
Beau Snider	Tulsa Union	DB	6-1	180	Senior
Marcus Whittaker	Dewar	LB	6-4	210	Senior

Specialists

Name	School	Pos.	Ht.	Wt.	Class
Justin Stone	OC Westmoore	K	5-7	185	Senior
Kevin Kester	Chickasha	P	5-10	162	Senior
George Delonia	Tulsa Rogers	KR	5-11	187	Senior

OKLAHOMA ALL-STATE FOOTBALL TEAM: 2000

FIRST TEAM

Offense

Name	School	Pos.	Ht.	Wt.	Class
Tyler Gooch	Tulsa Union	QB	6-0	185	Senior
Kejuan Jones	Jenks	RB	5-10	190	Senior
Chad Tsotigh	Moore	RB	6-3	195	Senior
Seymore Shaw	Shawnee	RB	6-0	210	Senior
Jerome Janet	Tulsa Union	WR	6-1	180	Senior
J. D. Runnels	MWC Carl Albert	TE	6-1	218	Junior
Dusty Gilles	Piedmont	OL	6-3	289	Senior
Derek Warehime	Choctaw	OL	6-2	278	Senior
Chris Miller	Stillwater	OL	6-1	260	Senior
Brent Caldwell	Tahlequah	OL	6-4	300	Senior
Tony Palmer	Midwest City	OL	6-3	305	Senior

Defense

Name	School	Pos.	Ht.	Wt.	Class
Jake Hager	Perry	DL	6-8	250	Senior
Brandon Lohr	Jenks	DL	6-1	230	Senior
Andrew Franklin	Lawton Eisenhower	DL	6-3	220	Senior
Brent Watson	Moore	LB	6-1	215	Senior
Josh Dupree	Tulsa Union	LB	5-11	205	Senior
Michael Wilson	Tulsa Washington	LB	6-2	215	Senior
Erick Warren	Poteau	LB	5-9	190	Senior
Bobby Klinck	Jenks	DB	5-11	190	Senior
Avery Shine	Eufaula	DB	6-0	187	Senior
Patrick Cobbs	Tecumseh	DB	5-9	180	Senior
Paul Duren	Del City	DB	6-1	205	Senior

Specialists

Name	School	Pos.	Ht.	Wt.	Class
A. J. Haglund	El Reno	K	5-7	151	Senior
Josh Fields	Stillwater	P	6-2	210	Senior
Marshell Chiles	El Reno	KR	5-10	205	Senior

OKLAHOMA ALL-STATE FOOTBALL TEAM: 2000

SECOND TEAM

Offense

Name	School	Pos.	Ht.	Wt.	Class
Paul Smith	Deer Creek	QB	6-2	168	Soph.
Corey Spotwood	Crooked Oak	RB	5-10	205	Senior
Alfred Jenkins	Lawton Eisenhower	RB	5-10	165	Senior
Santee Jackson	MWC Carl Albert	RB	5-11	205	Senior
Derek Amyx	Deer Creek	WR	5-10	175	Senior
Andrew Fleck	Edmond Santa Fe	TE	6-4	240	Senior
Danny Brown	Midwest City	OL	5-10	260	Senior
Joe Vaughn	Del City	OL	6-2	265	Senior
Matt Wakefield	El Reno	OL	6-5	250	Senior
Chris Hilton	Seminole	OL	6-2	280	Senior
Chris Cobbs	Comanche	OL	6-4	268	Senior

Defense

Name	School	Pos.	Ht.	Wt.	Class
Donnie Richardson	Clinton	DL	6-1	290	Senior
Trey Holloway	OC Heritage Hall	DL	6-2	270	Senior
Charlie Ward	Lawton	DL	6-1	195	Senior
Casey Hicks	Roland	LB	5-11	195	Senior
Jared Bowling	Jenks	LB	6-2	215	Senior
Russell Dennison	Weatherford	LB	6-4	220	Senior
Evan Helvey	Edmond North	LB	6-3	240	Senior
Chase Holland	OC Heritage Hall	DB	6-1	190	Senior
Kenneth West	OC Star Spencer	DB	6-1	190	Senior
Jowahn Poteat	Ardmore	DB	6-1	185	Senior
Brandon Barker	Clinton	DB	6-2	175	Senior

Specialists

Name	School	Pos.	Ht.	Wt.	Class
David Carlton	Tulsa Bishop Kelley	K	6-0	170	Senior
Mark Holata	Morris	P	6-2	235	Senior
Darnell Stephens	Midwest City	KR	6-3	190	Senior

OKLAHOMA ALL-STATE FOOTBALL TEAM: 2000

THIRD TEAM

Offense

Name	School	Pos.	Ht.	Wt.	Class
Mike Hale	Moore	QB	6-3	220	Senior
Bennie Clayborn	Apache	RB	5-10	195	Senior
Rock Rodebush	Ada	RB	6-1	183	Senior
Kolby Simpson	Tonkawa	RB	5-7	175	Senior
Leonard Jones	Stillwater	WR	6-0	190	Senior
Colt Allison	Washington	TE	6-3	230	Senior
Charles Cartile	Collinsville	OL	6-6	350	Senior
Kellen Davis	Stigler	OL	6-4	240	Senior
Tito Griffin	Lawton	OL	6-1	230	Senior
Brent Banks	Pawnee	OL	6-3	290	Senior
Jarod Mason	Moore	OL	6-2	290	Senior

Defense

Name	School	Pos.	Ht.	Wt.	Class
Ete Mowarin	Tulsa Memorial	DL	6-1	280	Senior
Grady Davis	Norman	DL	6-6	225	Senior
Nathan Dobbs	Sallisaw	DL	6-2	220	Senior
James Burch	Lindsay	LB	5-11	200	Senior
Keith Edwards	Lawton Eisenhower	LB	5-11	215	Senior
Jeff Bradley	Norman North	LB	5-11	205	Senior
Sam Kennon	Putnam North	LB	6-4	221	Senior
Melvin Watts	Davis	DB	5-8	155	Senior
Britton Langdon	Edmond North	DB	6-0	185	Senior
Jace Sherrell	Putnam North	DB	5-11	180	Senior
Andre Johnson	Chickasha	DB	5-10	180	Senior

Specialists

Name	School	Pos.	Ht.	Wt.	Class
Ben Brosey	Putnam North	K	6-0	175	Senior
Rodney Skinner	Clinton	P	6-0	170	Senior
Kevin McKenzie	Chickasha	KR	5-10	195	Senior

Cecil Eugene Reinke was born and grew up in Clinton, Oklahoma. He attended Nance grade school and Wilson Jr. High School. He was graduated from Clinton High School with the Class of 1952. While in high school, he was a for three years a member of the Clinton High School football team, the Red Tornadoes; he served four years on the Student Council; served as the Representative-At-Large to Clinton's Original Teen Town; and was a co-editor of the high school newspaper, the *Whirlwind.* Upon graduation, he was awarded the Creative Writing Award presented by the Literary Department of the Allied Arts Club.

He attended North Dakota State University from September 1952 to June 1955. He graduated from the University of North Dakota, School of Arts and Sciences, in 1956, and from the University of North Dakota School of Law, awarded the degree Juris Doctor, "with distinction," in 1959. He served as an Associate Editor of the North Dakota Law Review and was elected to the Order of the Coif. He earned a Master of Science in Environmental Management, 1977, from the University of Houston at Clear Lake, meriting election to Phi Kappa Phi. He served as a Senior Executive Fellow, John F. Kennedy School of Government, Harvard University, 1986. He earned a Ph.D. at Portland State University, Portland, Oregon, School of Urban and Public Affairs, 1991.

He served forty years as a lawyer with the United States Army Corps of Engineers. He also served as a part time instructor at Galveston College, Galveston, Texas, and at the University of Houston, Clear Lake, and at Concordia University in Portland, Oregon. Now retired from Federal service, he continues teaching at Concordia University, while working as a writer.

Reader Assistance Required

This effort to identify all of the players on Oklahoma high school All-State football teams of the twentieth century, selected by *The Daily Oklahoman,* now designated *The Oklahoman,* is incomplete, and in need of assistance. Numerous All-State football players are listed herein by surnames, last names, only, their given names still to be added. Hopefully, surely, there are supporters and fans of Oklahoma high school football that know some of the given names that are missing. Readers who know given names—first names, middle names, and/ or nicknames—of players listed in this book by last names only are invited, requested, to advise the author by traditional mail: Cecil Eugene Reinke, 7805 SW Terwilliger Boulevard, Portland, Oregon 97219, or by E-mail: cecilreinke@ comcast.net. Assistance provided will be sincerely appreciated.

C. E. R.